BEDROOMS OF THE FALLEN

BEDROOMS OF THE FALLEN

Ashley Gilbertson

WITH A FOREWORD BY PHILIP GOUREVITCH

The University of Chicago Press   Chicago and London

Ashley Gilbertson is a photographer and the author of *Whiskey Tango Foxtrot: A Photographer's Chronicle of the Iraq War* (2007). His photographs have appeared in the *New Yorker*, the *New York Times Magazine*, *Stern*, and other publications. His work is included in the collections of major museums throughout the United States, Europe, and Australia. Among numerous honors, Gilbertson won the prestigious Robert Capa Gold Medal for his photographs of the battle of Falluja and in 2012 was awarded a National Magazine Award for a *New York Times Magazine* extract from the *Bedrooms of the Fallen* project.

Philip Gourevitch is a journalist, writer, and former editor of the *Paris Review*. He is the author of *We Wish to Inform You That Tomorrow We Will Be Killed with Our Families: Stories from Rwanda* and *A Cold Case* and coauthor of *The Ballad of Abu Ghraib*.

The University of Chicago Press, Chicago 60637
The University of Chicago Press, Ltd., London

Printed in Canada

23 22 21 20 19 18 17 16 15 14   1 2 3 4 5

ISBN-13: 978-0-226-06686-8 (cloth)
ISBN-13: 978-0-226-13511-3 (e-book)
DOI: 10.7208/chicago/9780226135113.001.0001

Library of Congress Cataloging-in-Publication Data

Gilbertson, Ashley, author.
Bedrooms of the fallen / Ashley Gilbertson ; with a foreword by Philip Gourevitch.
pages cm
ISBN 978-0-226-06686-8 (cloth : alk. paper)
ISBN 978-0-226-13511-3 (e-book)
1. Iraq War, 2003-2011—Casualties—Pictorial works.
2. Afghan War, 2001-—Casualties—Pictorial works. I. Title.
DS79.767.C37G55 2014
956.7044'36—dc23
2013043357

∞ This paper meets the requirements of ANSI/NISO Z39.48-1992 (Permanence of Paper).

For Billy Miller, who died in my place. I'm sorry.
and
For Joanna, always.

CONTENTS

FOREWORD

Philip Gourevitch

Imagine Chicago empty. Picture the city perfectly intact, and nobody in it. Not a soul, we say, to describe such abandonment. Empty, we say, deserted. And yes, there would be nobody there—no bodies to be seen—but the souls of the missing people would permeate the place they'd left behind. All those buildings full of rooms, all those rooms full of stuff—and the rooms and the stuff brimming with the presence of absent life. You would have to visit everybody's room to feel the enormity of the loss, an impossible mission, and an impossible feeling. Chicago is a city of 2.7 million people, and that is why I'm asking you to imagine all of them gone—because 2.7 million is the number of men and women in America's military services who have died in our wars since the country took up arms to win its independence on the battlefield.

"At the close of that struggle," Abraham Lincoln said of the American Revolution, "nearly every adult male had been a participator in some of its scenes. The consequence was that of those scenes, in the form of a husband, a father, a son, or a brother, a living history was to be found in every family—a history bearing the indubitable testimonies of its own authenticity, in the limbs mangled, in the scars of wounds received, in the midst of the very scenes related—a history, too, that could be read and understood alike by all, the wise and the ignorant, the learned and the unlearned."

The same could be said, in turn, of Lincoln's war. There were more American military deaths in the Civil War than in all our subsequent wars combined, and once again every American family knew its reality intimately. What's more, the image of that war was seared indelibly in the national memory by the advent of a new technology: photography. Never since has America fought a major war on its own soil, but wherever our troops have gone, cameras have followed them. War has been unimaginable without them.

Still, throughout the twentieth century, as pictures on film became the dominant medium through which we saw war, Americans maintained the sense of direct connection to our military that Abraham Lincoln remarked in the early days of the republic. In both World Wars, in Korea and Vietnam, conscription meant that every family in America should have a stake in its wars. That was the principle and to a large degree the practice. The draft insured, much better than all the cameras in the world, that the toll of war could not be made invisible.

That seems like ancient history now. With our retreat from Vietnam, we also retreated from the idea of a popular army. The military became the business of a small, self-selecting subset of the nation, whose charge it is to fight so that the rest of us should never know war. And perhaps this arrangement has succeeded too well. Since September 11, 2001, America has been engaged—along with our NATO allies—in two of the longest, most grimly grinding wars in our history. Military families have endured every conceivable strain and anguish. But for the vast majority of us, these wars are not just overseas, they are completely foreign: they do not hit us where we live.

Nearly seven thousand Americans have died in Afghanistan and Iraq, and more than fifty thousand have been wounded. This loss has received only faint and fleeting official recognition. Mourning is treated as a private matter, as if these dead belonged only to their comrades and kin, and not to us all. For many years, the government, fearful of a negative effect on fragile public opinion, forbade the publication not only of images of combat casualties, but even of flag-draped caskets coming home. But isn't it a dishonor to the dead to try to hide them from the nation they served?

The need to see America's twenty-first-century war dead, and to make them seen—to give their absence presence—has consumed Ashley Gilbertson for much of the past decade. The initial impulse was purely personal. While he was working as a photojournalist in Iraq, a Marine stepped forward to protect him, and was killed; and Gilbertson was haunted by the feeling that Lance Corporal Billy Miller, in doing what he understood as his duty, had died for him.

In the appalling immediacy of his experience, Gilbertson came to recognize a general truth: that, like it or not, these wars really are ours—they implicate us—and when our military men and women die in far-off lands, they do so in our name. He wanted to depict what it means that they are gone. Photographs of the fallen, or of their coffins or their graves, don't tell us that. But the places they came from and were supposed to go back to—the places they left empty—do tell us. So, to picture death, Gilbertson decided to picture how and where the dead had lived. He set about photographing their bedrooms, many of which had been preserved by their families in much the same spirit that Gilbertson preserved them with his camera: as memorials.

Some rooms are starkly spare; some explode with personality. There is a lot of sports gear and memorabilia; there are not a lot of books. There are rooms that belonged to people blown up by IEDs, and rooms that belonged to people who were blown up by suicide bombers. The only room that is in real disarray—bedclothes scrambled, belongings spilling from bags—belonged to Private Danny Chen, who took his own life in Afghanistan. Seen all together, Gilbertson's photographs defy any effort to seek in a room's furnishings an echo of its former occupant's fate. Their power lies in reminding us of the disconnect between life and death. One of the most elaborately and carefully kept rooms, nearly every inch of which is lovingly decorated, also belonged to a soldier defeated by the enemy within: Specialist Ryan Yurchison, who returned traumatized from Iraq, and took an overdose.

You can spend a great deal of time visiting each of the rooms in these photographs, studying their endless particularities. Gilbertson found these rooms all over the map: in cities, suburbs, and hinterland, scattered across the country. And since America's story is always bigger than America, and our losses in our recent wars have been shared with NATO partners, there are rooms here from the Isle of Mull in Scotland, from Versailles, France, and from Bitetto, Italy. But one thing that all the rooms here have in common is that they belonged to young people, people just out of high school, mostly, people well on their way to adulthood but still living in their parents' homes, sleeping in single beds, often with a teddy bear or two looking over them—like children. That is who we send to fight our wars for us, our children. Ashley Gilbertson is right: we should never lose sight of them.

BEDROOMS OF THE FALLEN

Air Force Airman First Class Carl L. Anderson Jr., 21, was killed by an IED on August 29, 2004, in Mosul, Iraq. He was from Georgetown, South Carolina. His bedroom was photographed in March 2009.

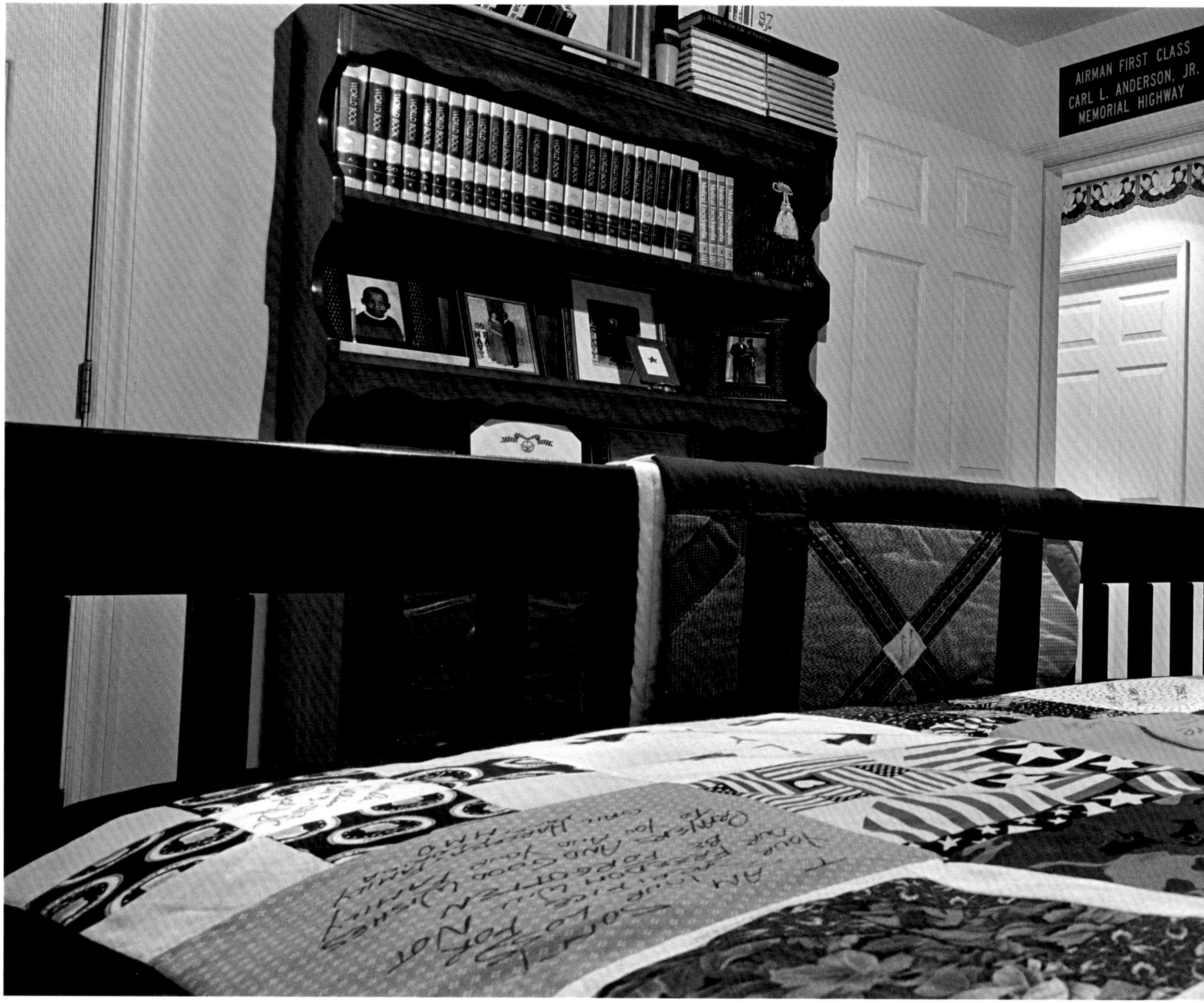

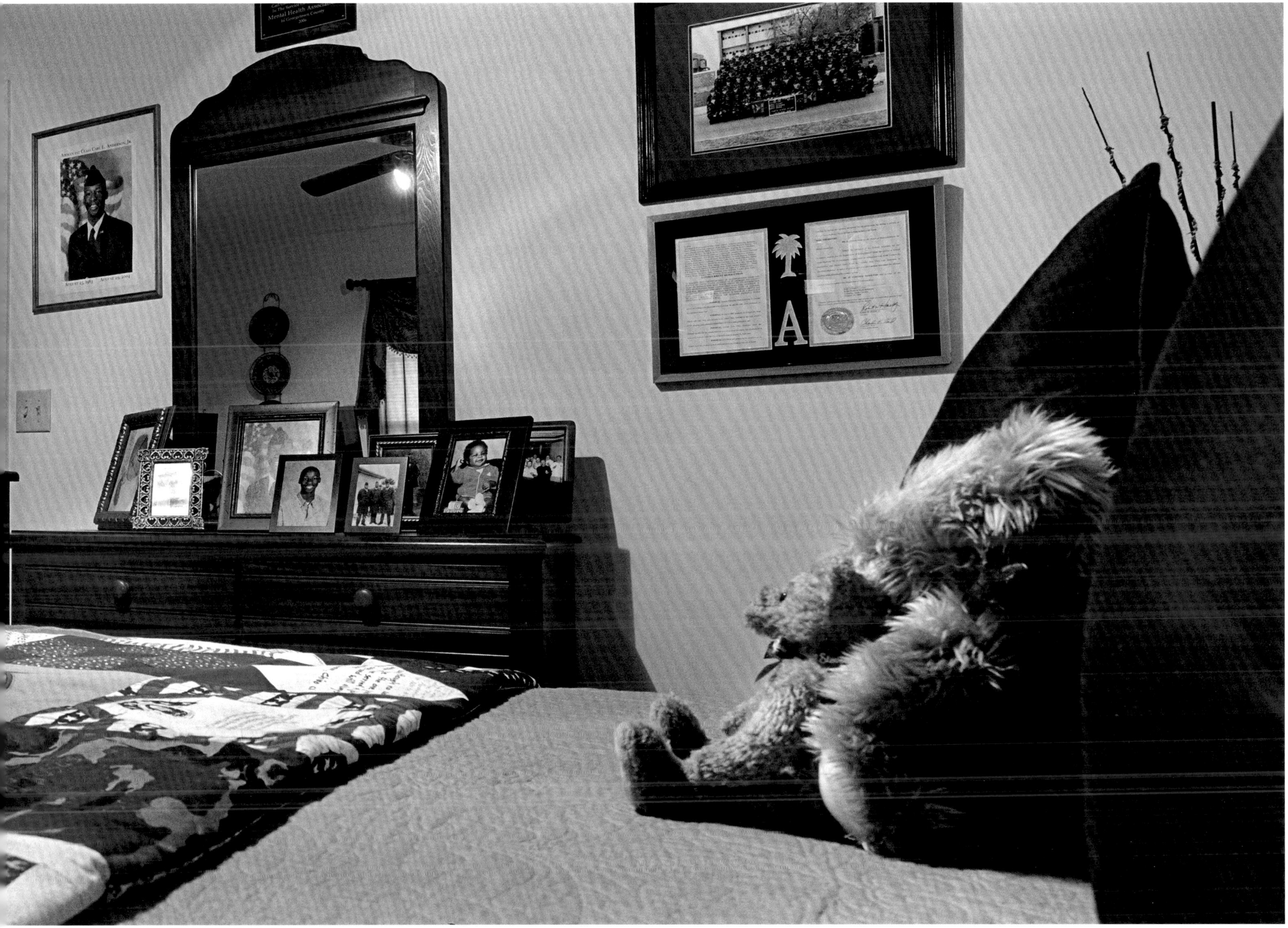
Mental Health Association

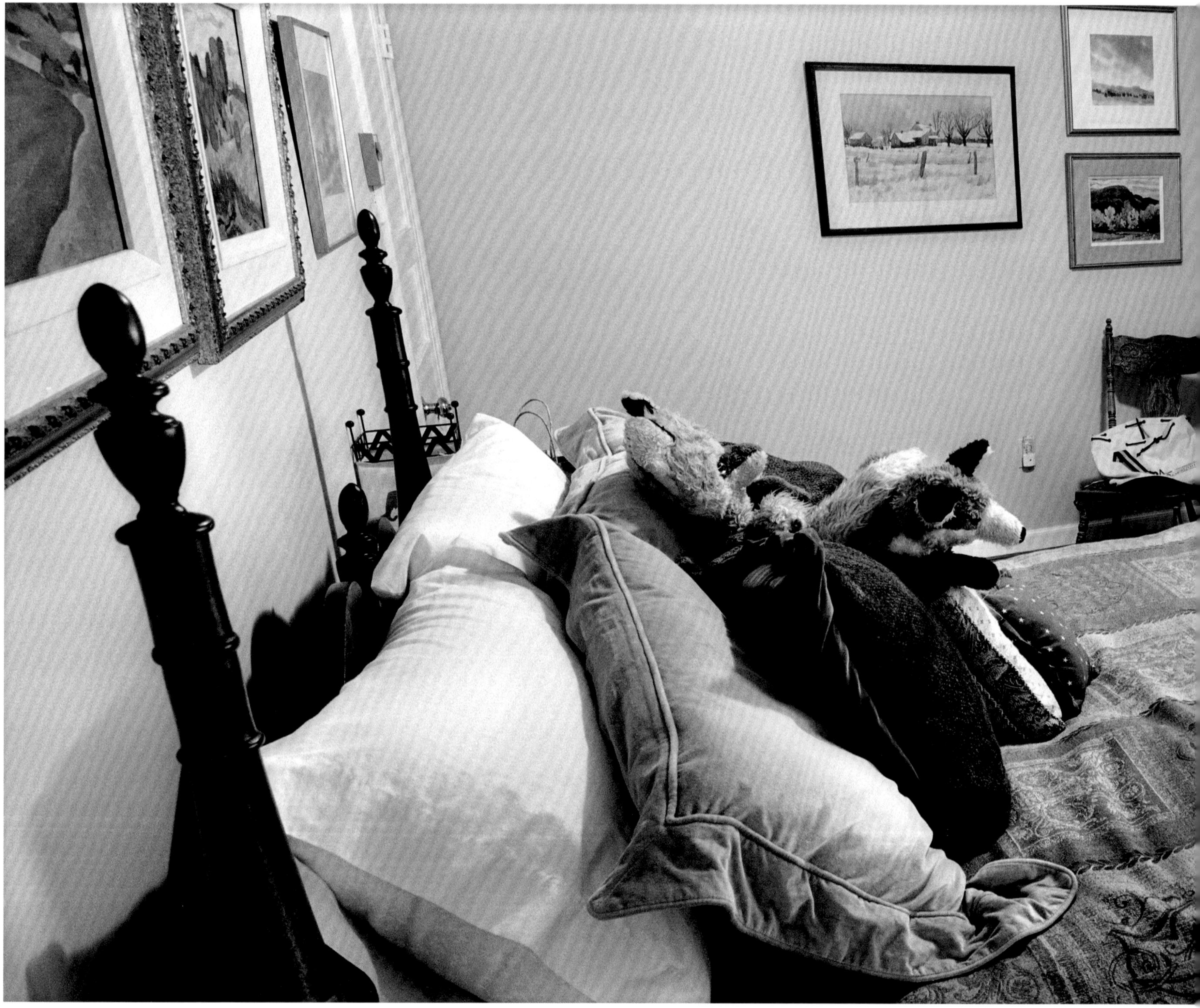

Marine Corporal Kirk J. Bosselmann, 21, was killed by small arms fire on November 27, 2004, in Falluja, Iraq. He was from Dickerson, Maryland. His bedroom was photographed in February 2010.

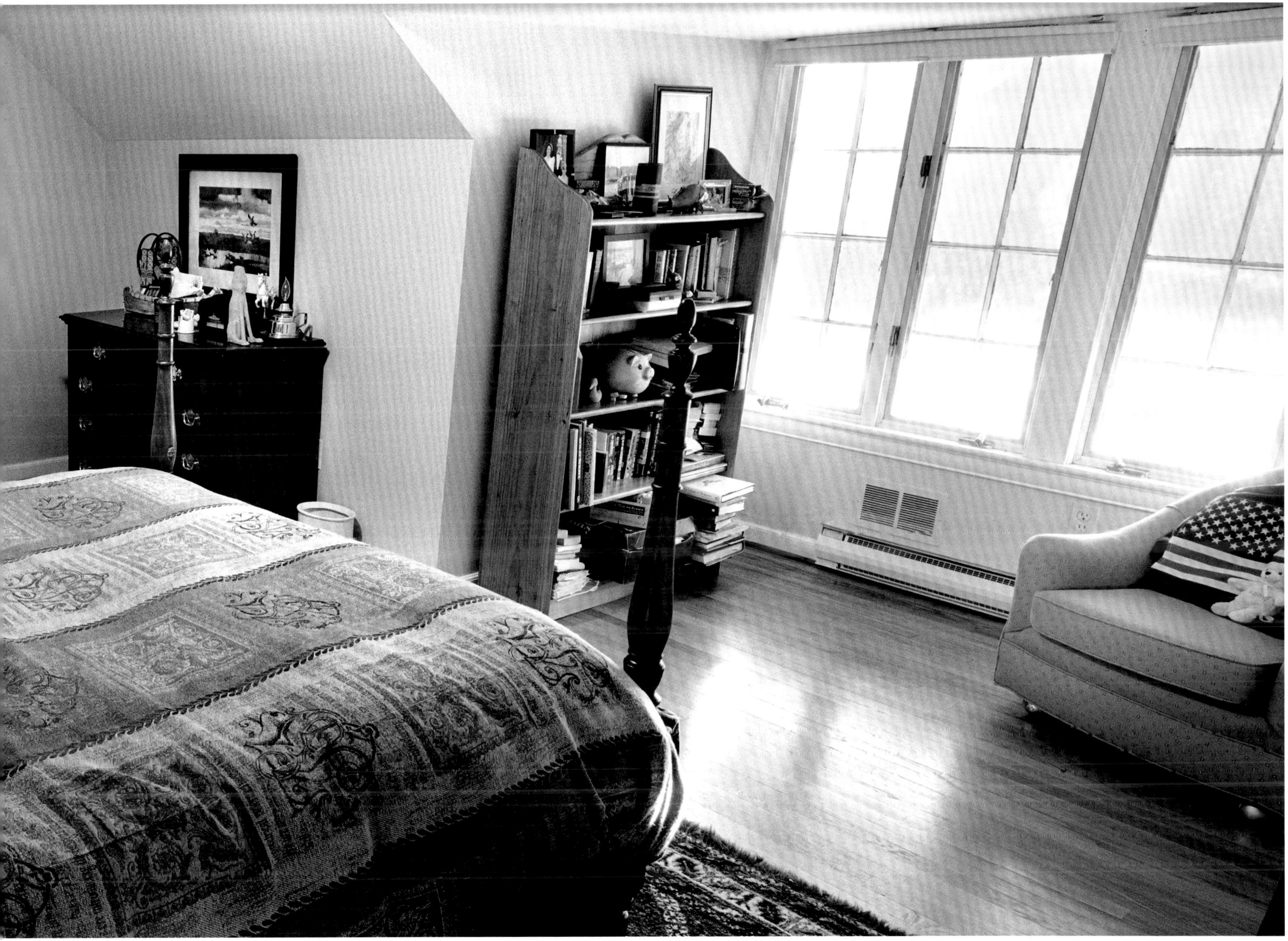

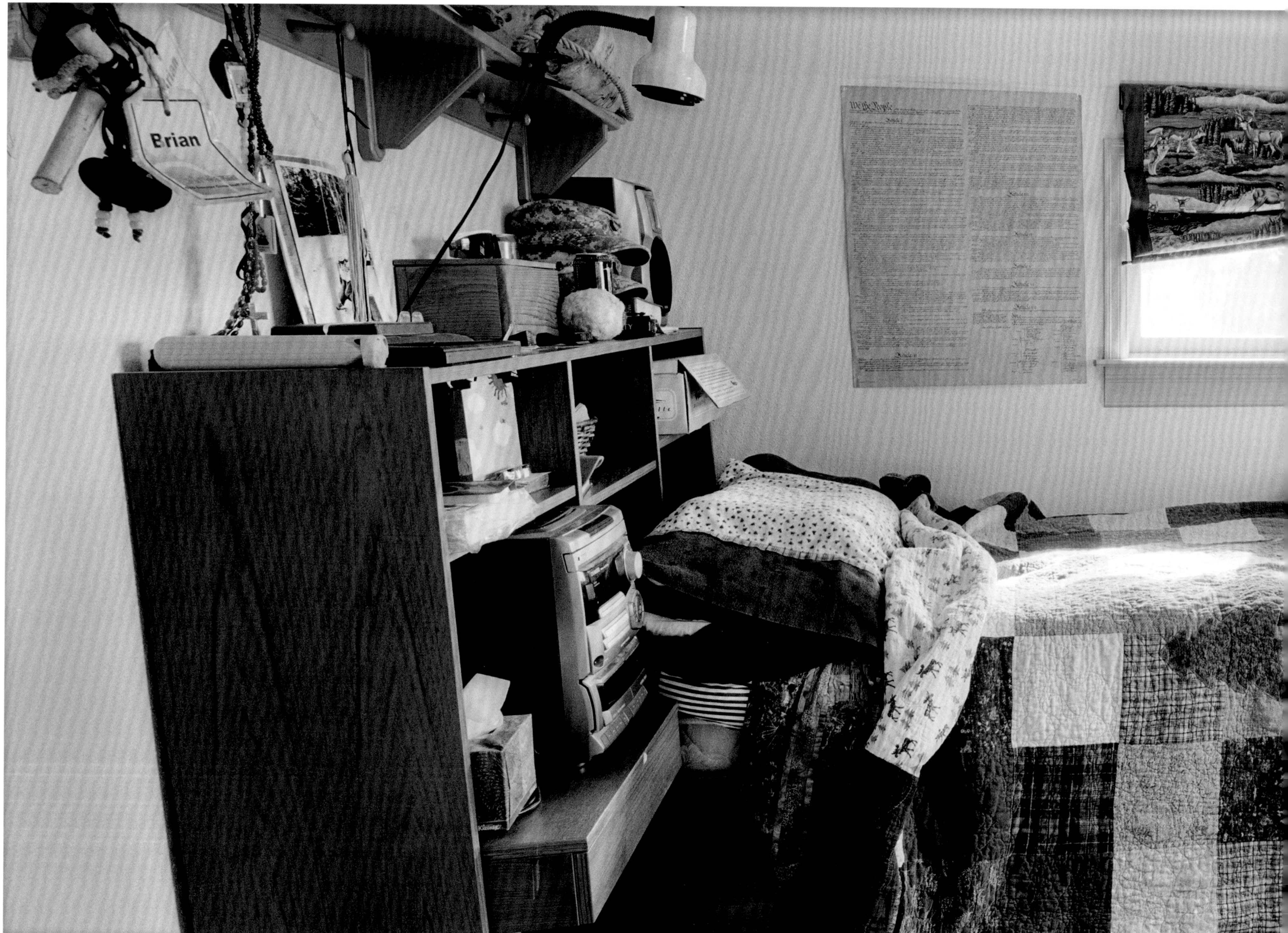
Brian
We the People

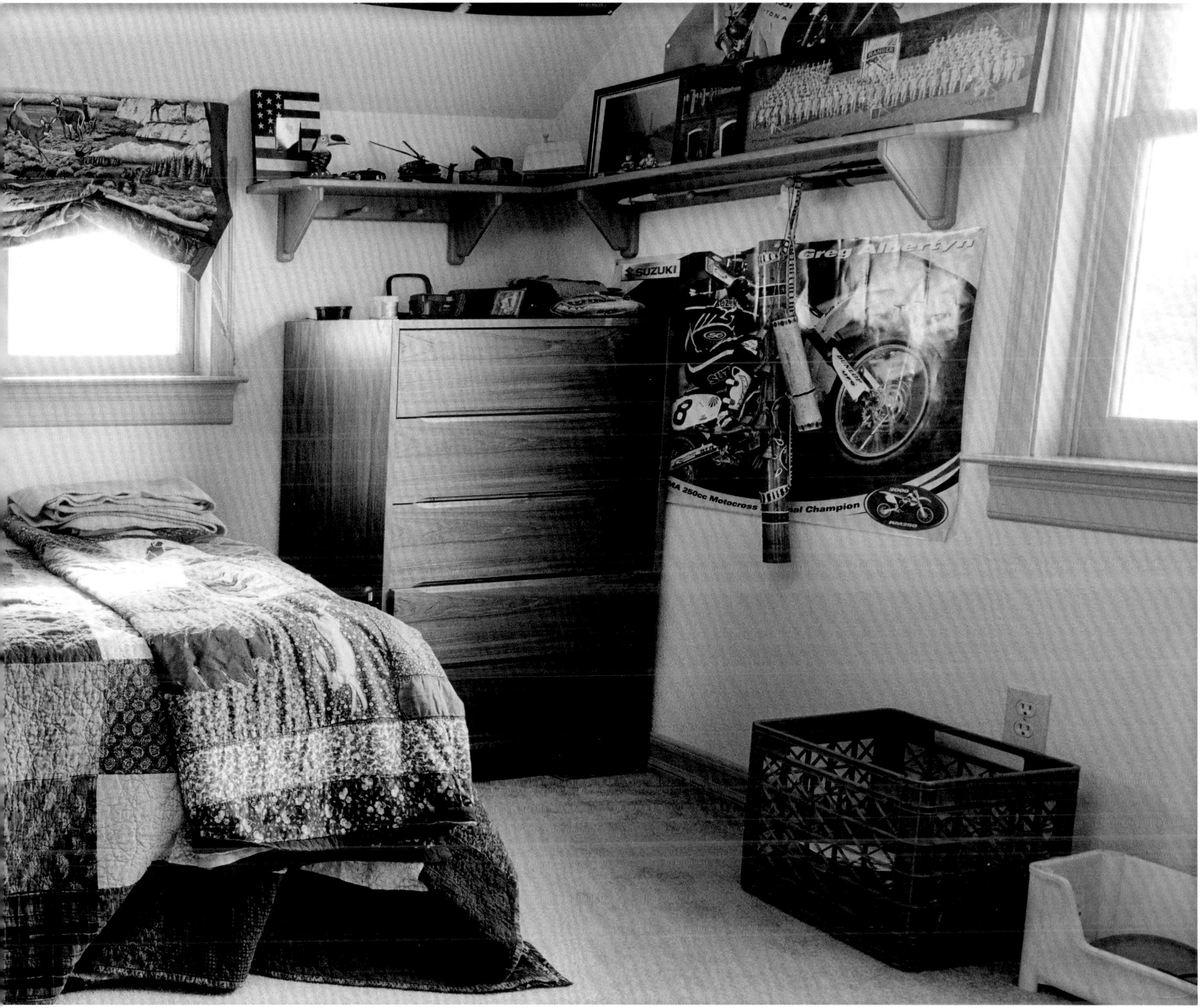

Army Lieutenant Brian N. Bradshaw, 24, was killed in an IED attack on June 25, 2009, in Kheyl, Afghanistan. He was from Steilacoom, Washington. His bedroom was photographed in February 2010.

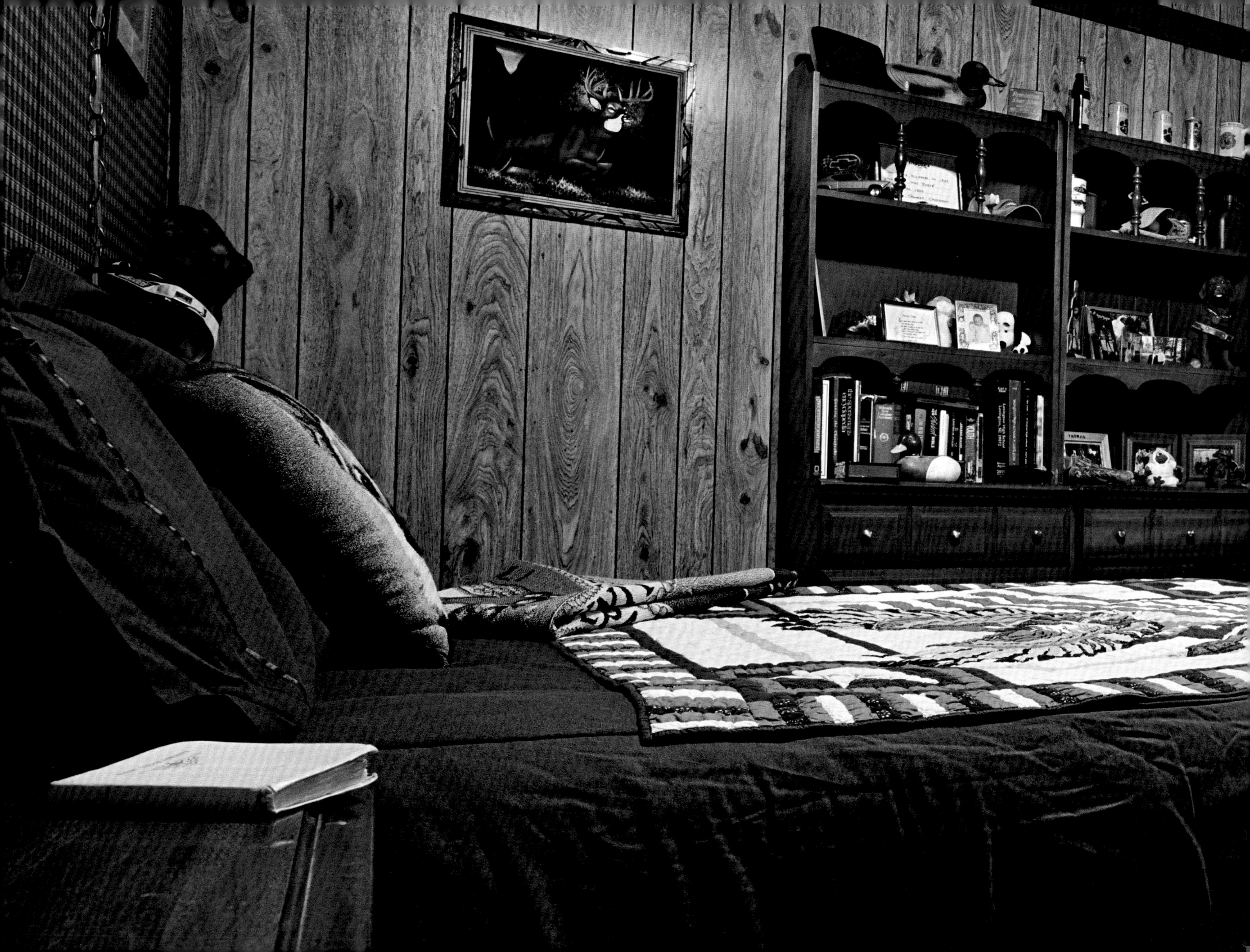

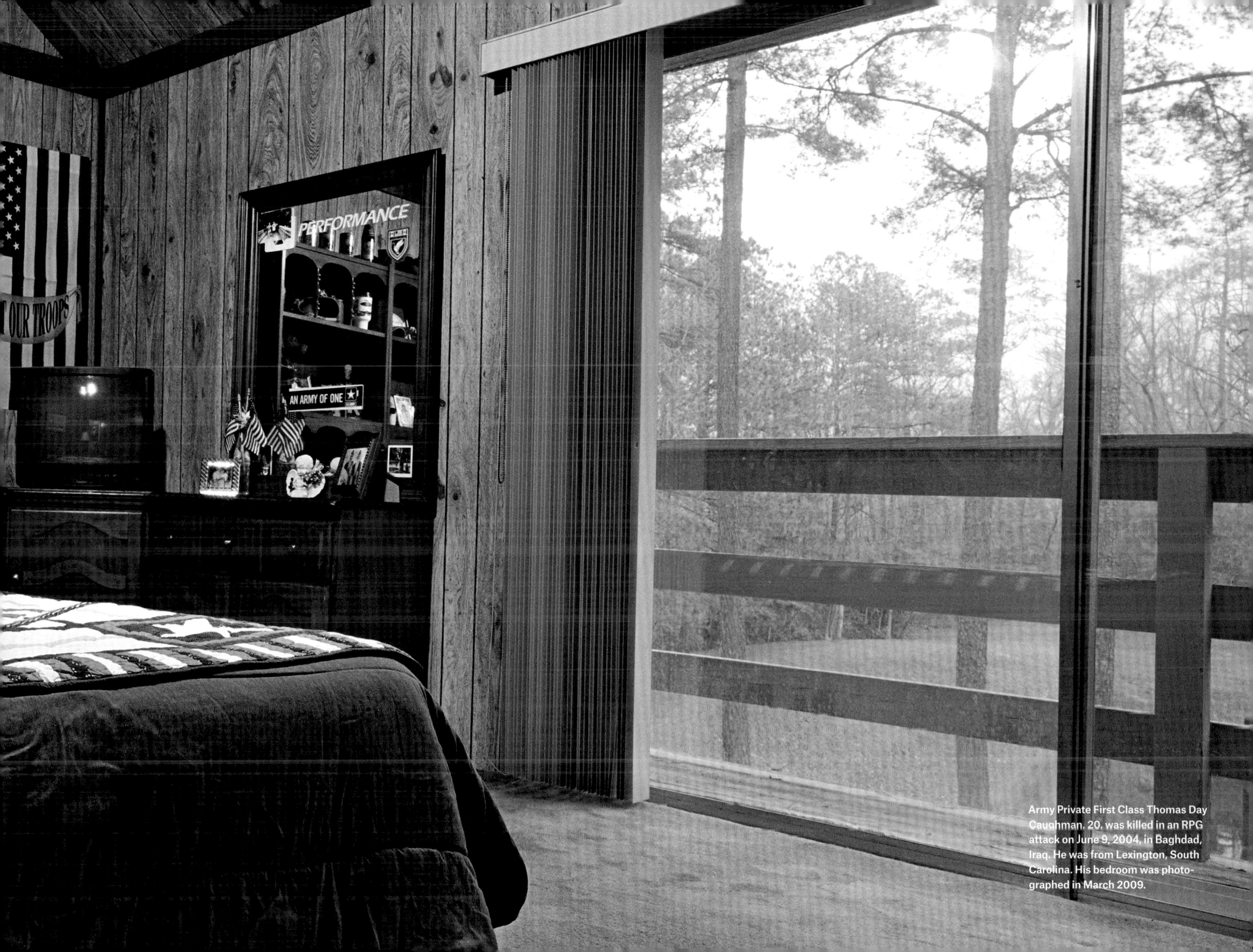

Army Private First Class Thomas Day Caughman, 20, was killed in an RPG attack on June 9, 2004, in Baghdad, Iraq. He was from Lexington, South Carolina. His bedroom was photographed in March 2009.

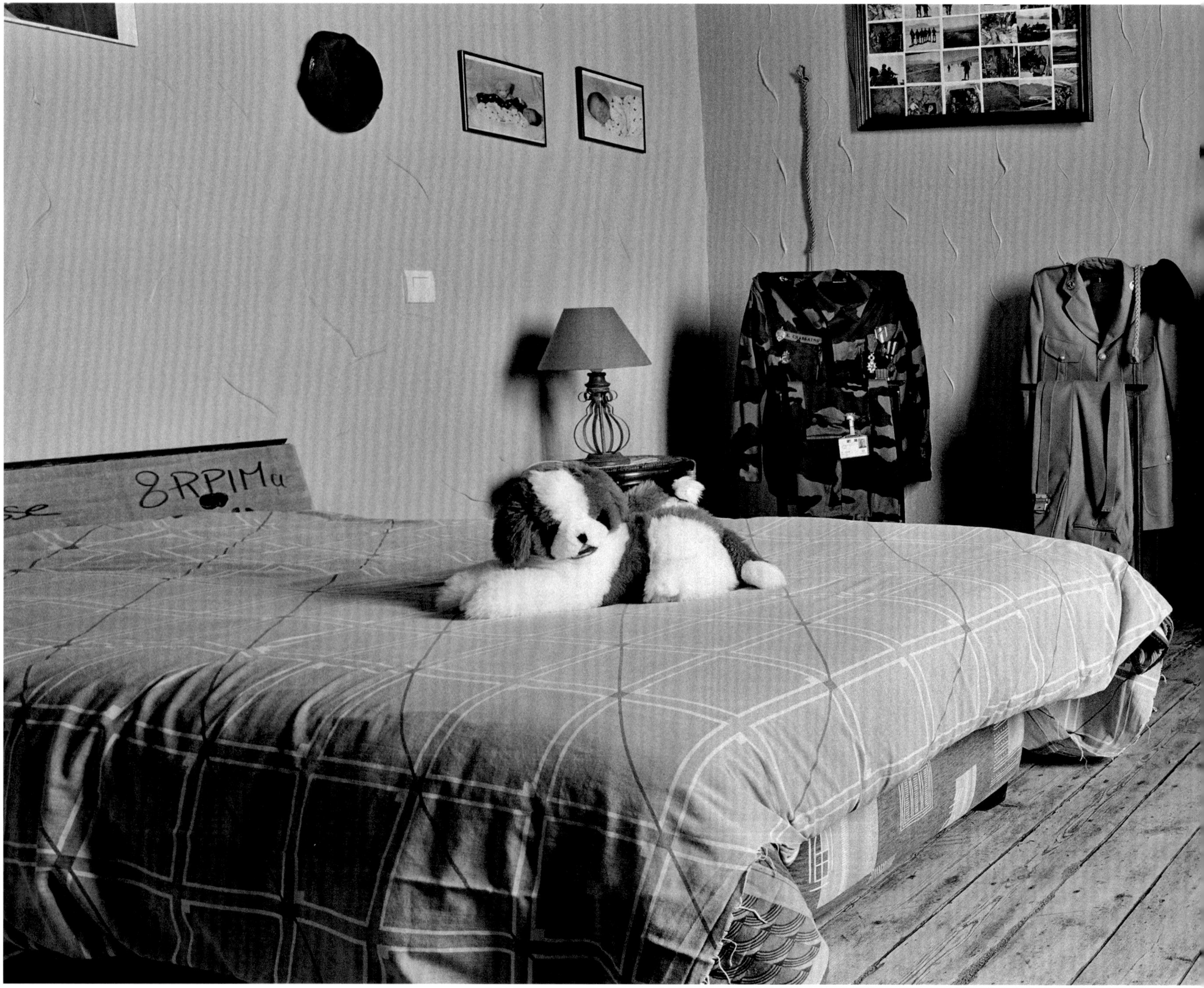

Marine Corporal Kevin Chassaing, 19, was killed in an ambush on August 18, 2008, in the Uzbin Valley, Afghanistan. He was from Couthures-sur-Garonne, in southwestern France. His bedroom was photographed in March 2011.

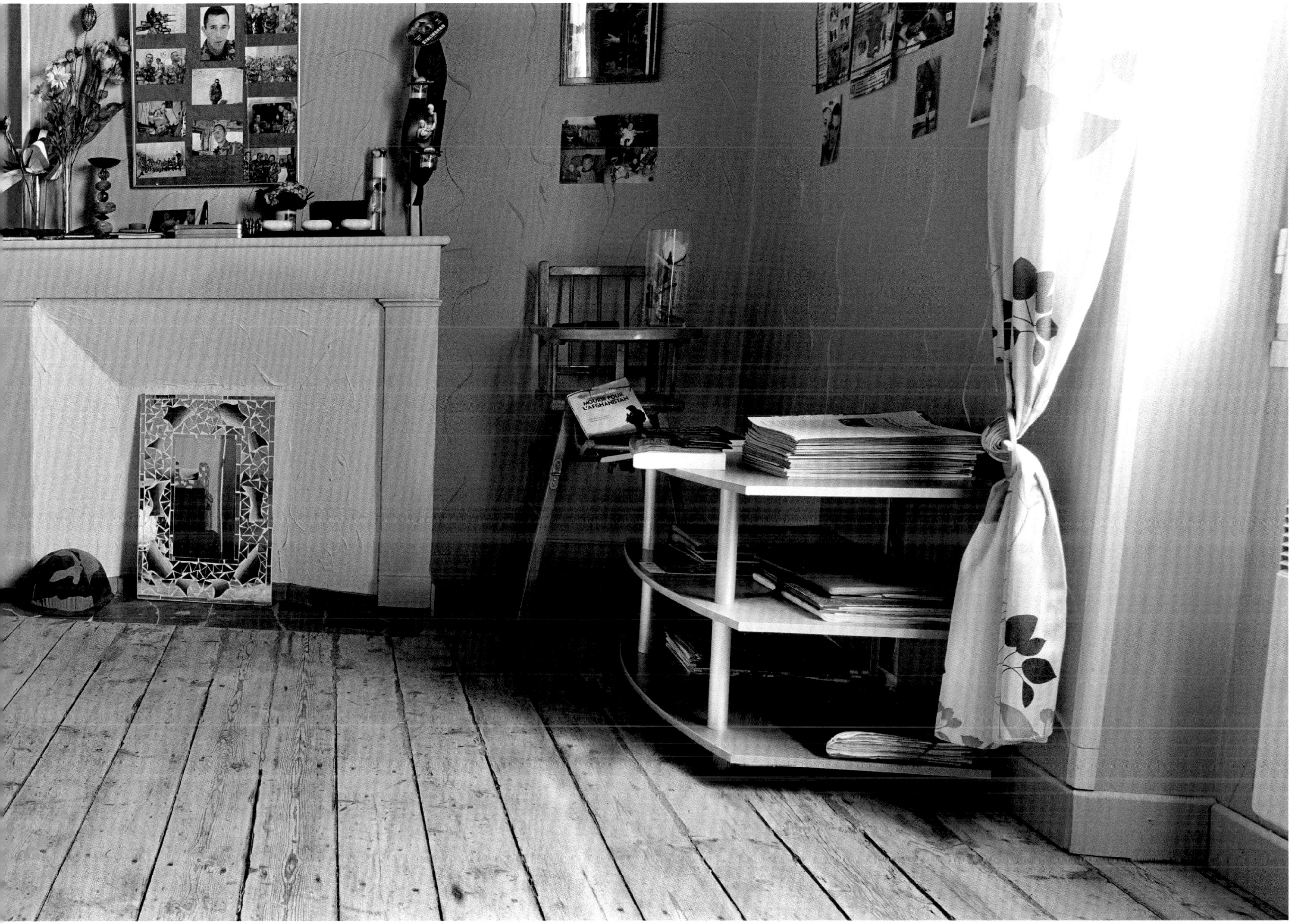
MOURIR POUR
L'AFGHANISTAN

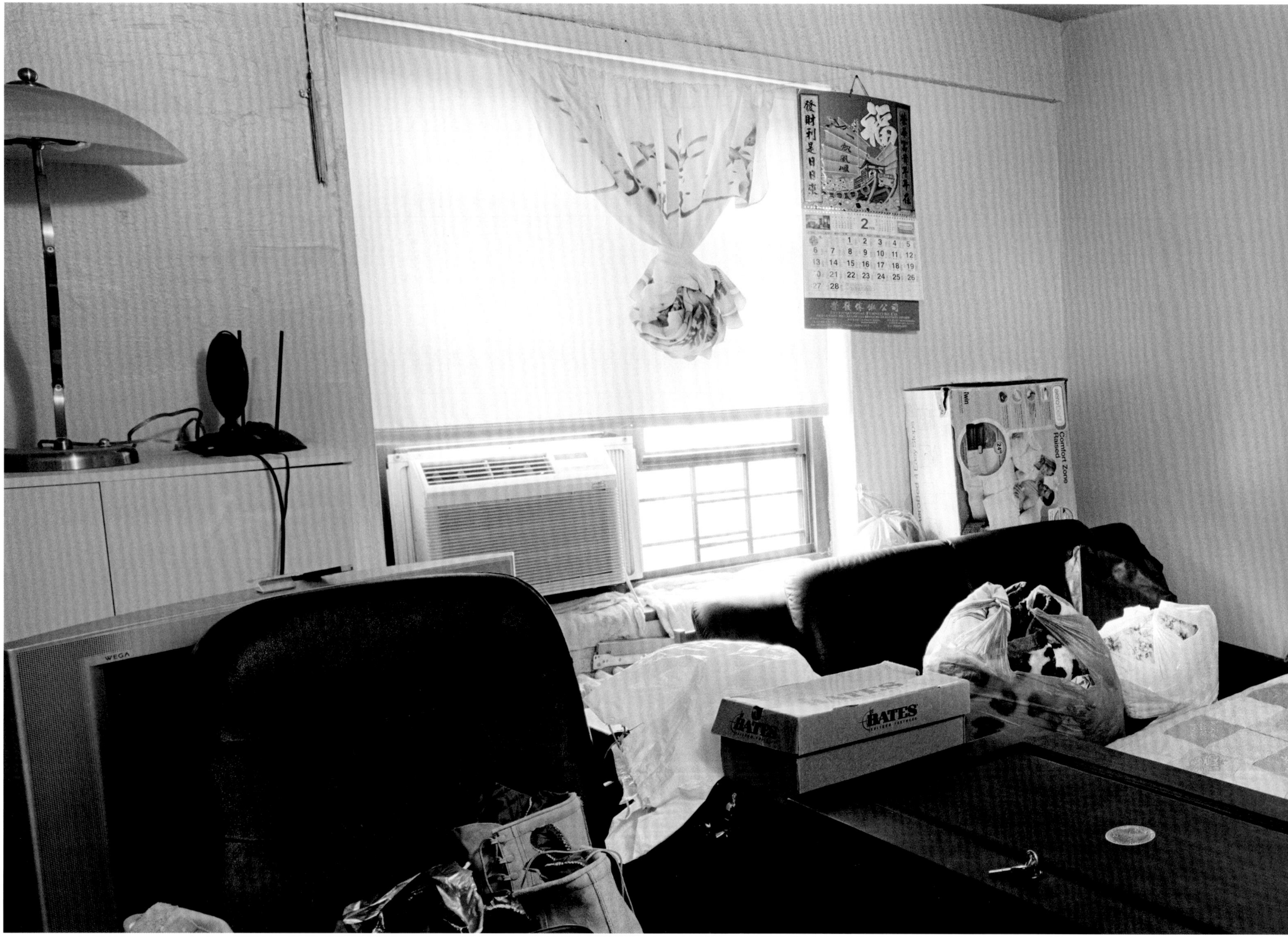
WEGA
BATES
Comfort Zone Raised

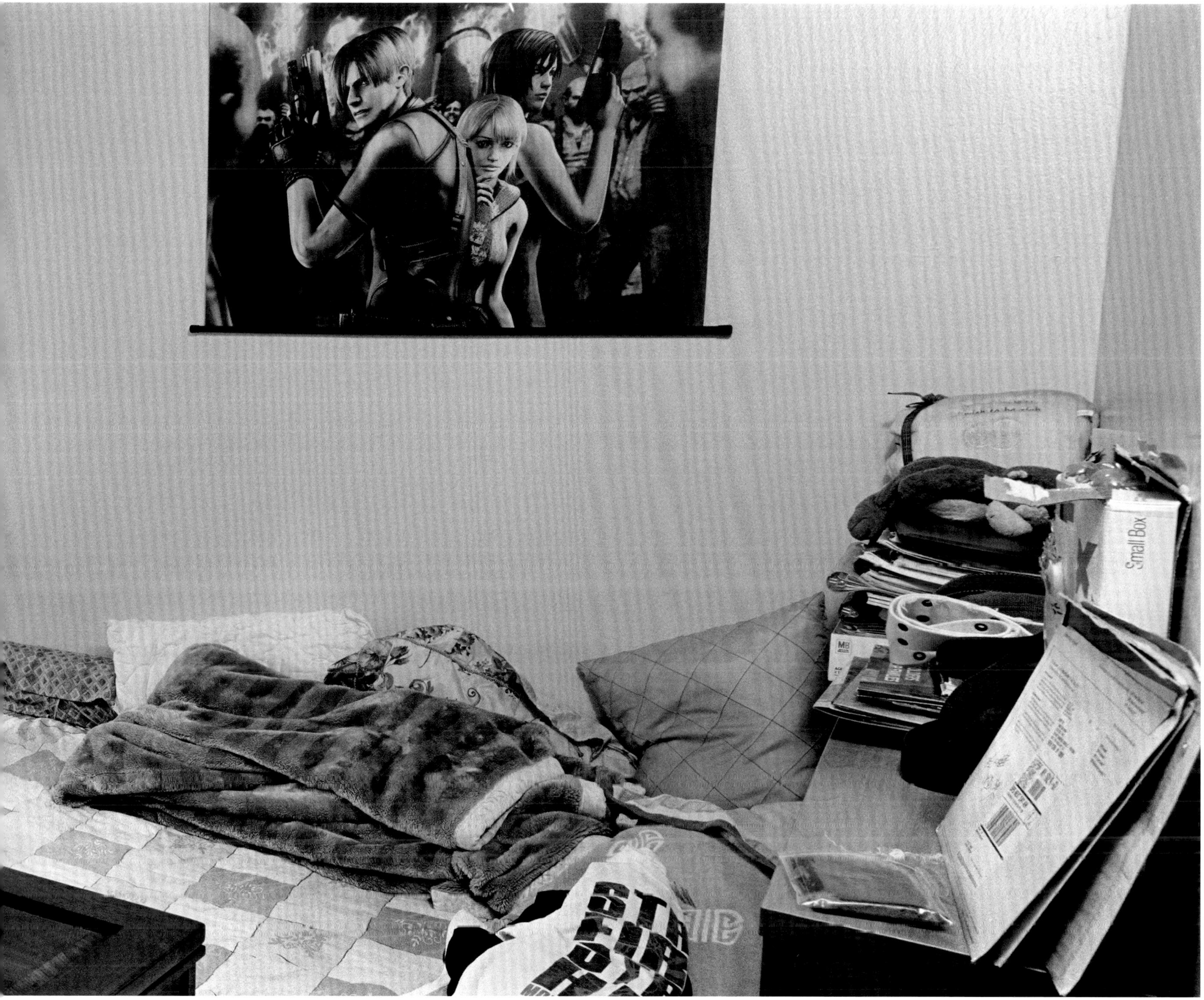

Private Danny Chen, 19, killed himself on October 3, 2011, in Kandahar province, Afghanistan. He was from Alphabet City, New York, New York. His bedroom was photographed in January 2012.

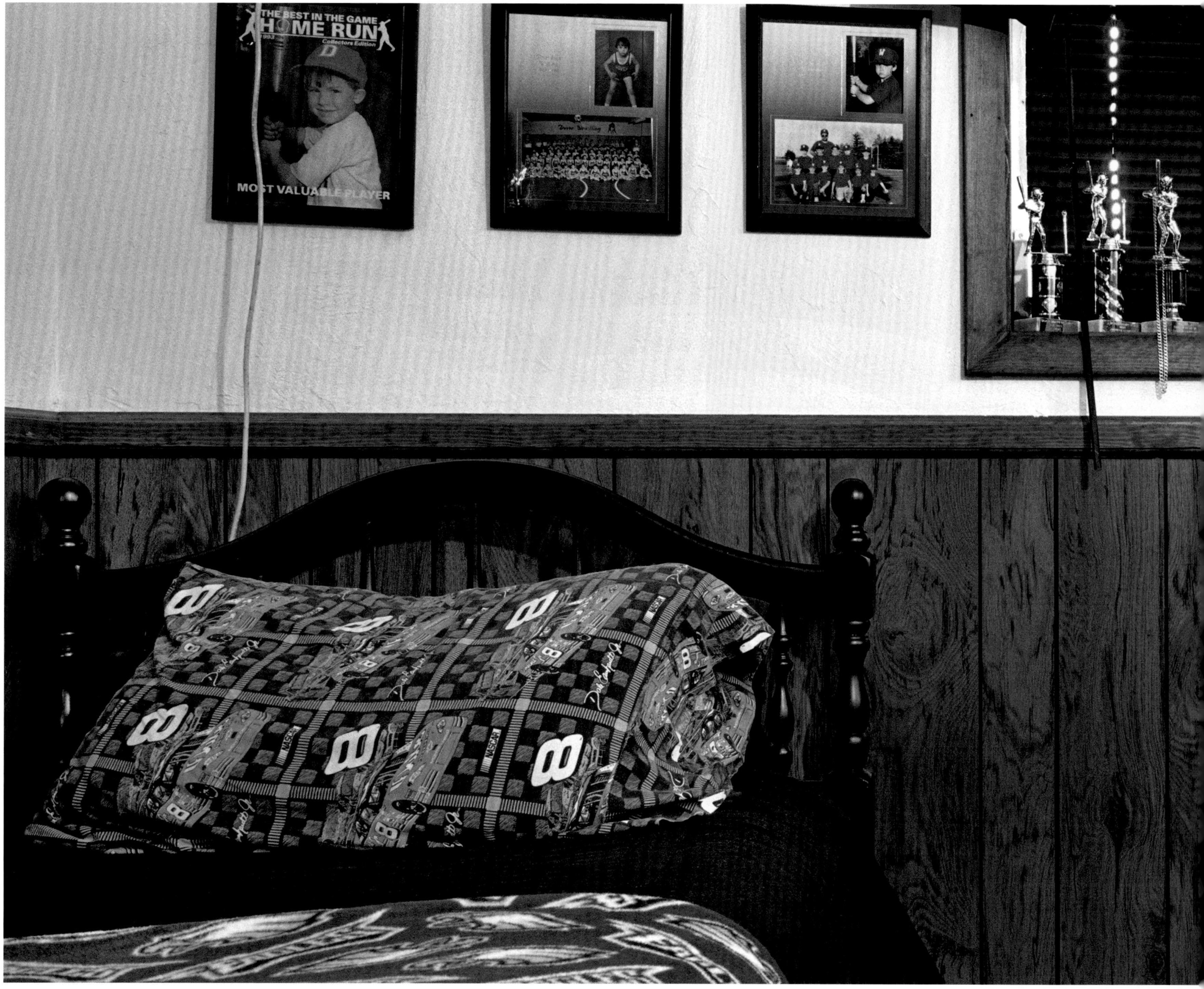

Army Specialist Zachary R. Clouser, 19, was killed by an IED on July 18, 2007, in Baghdad, Iraq. He was from Dover, Pennsylvania. His bedroom was photographed in September 2007.

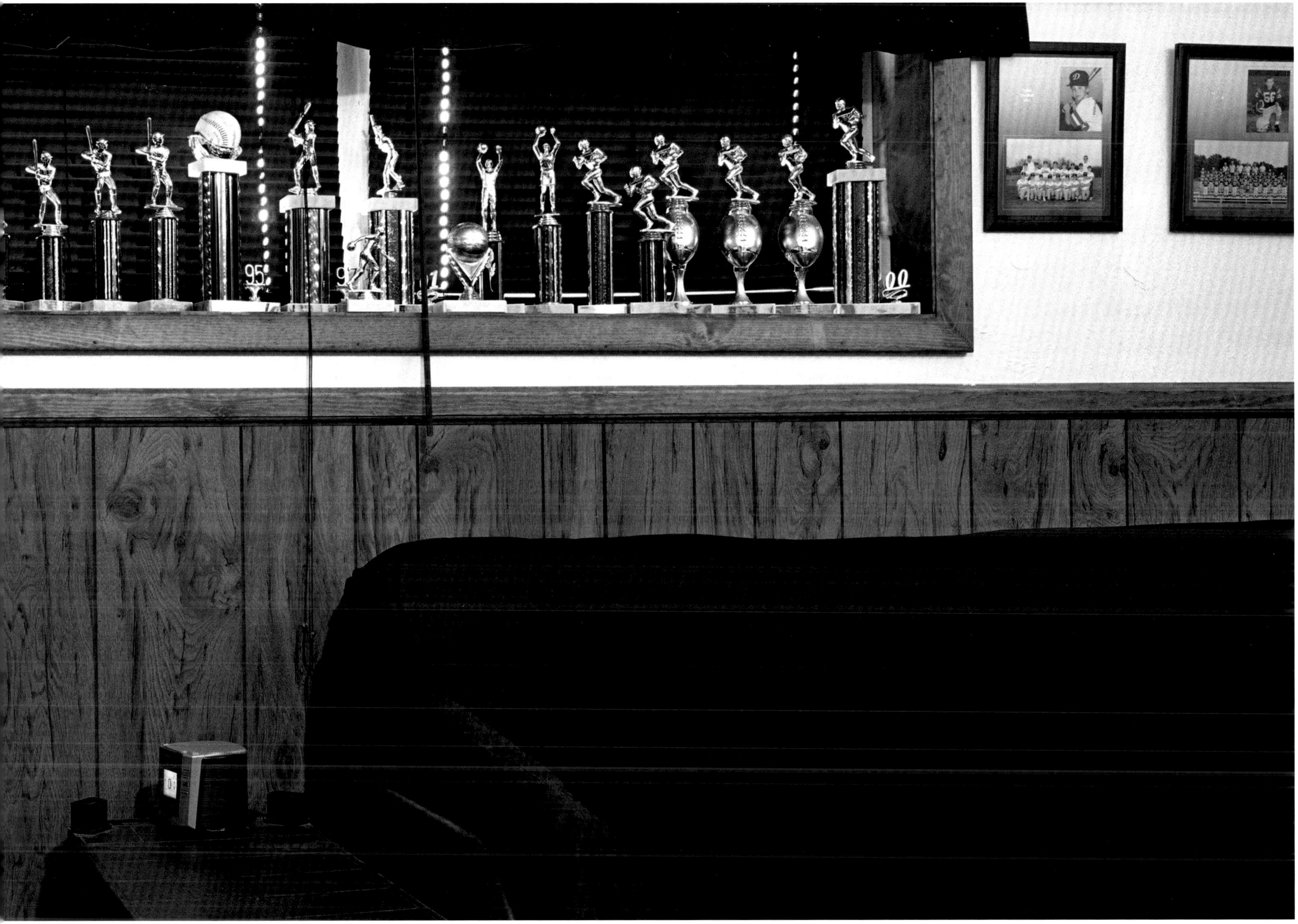

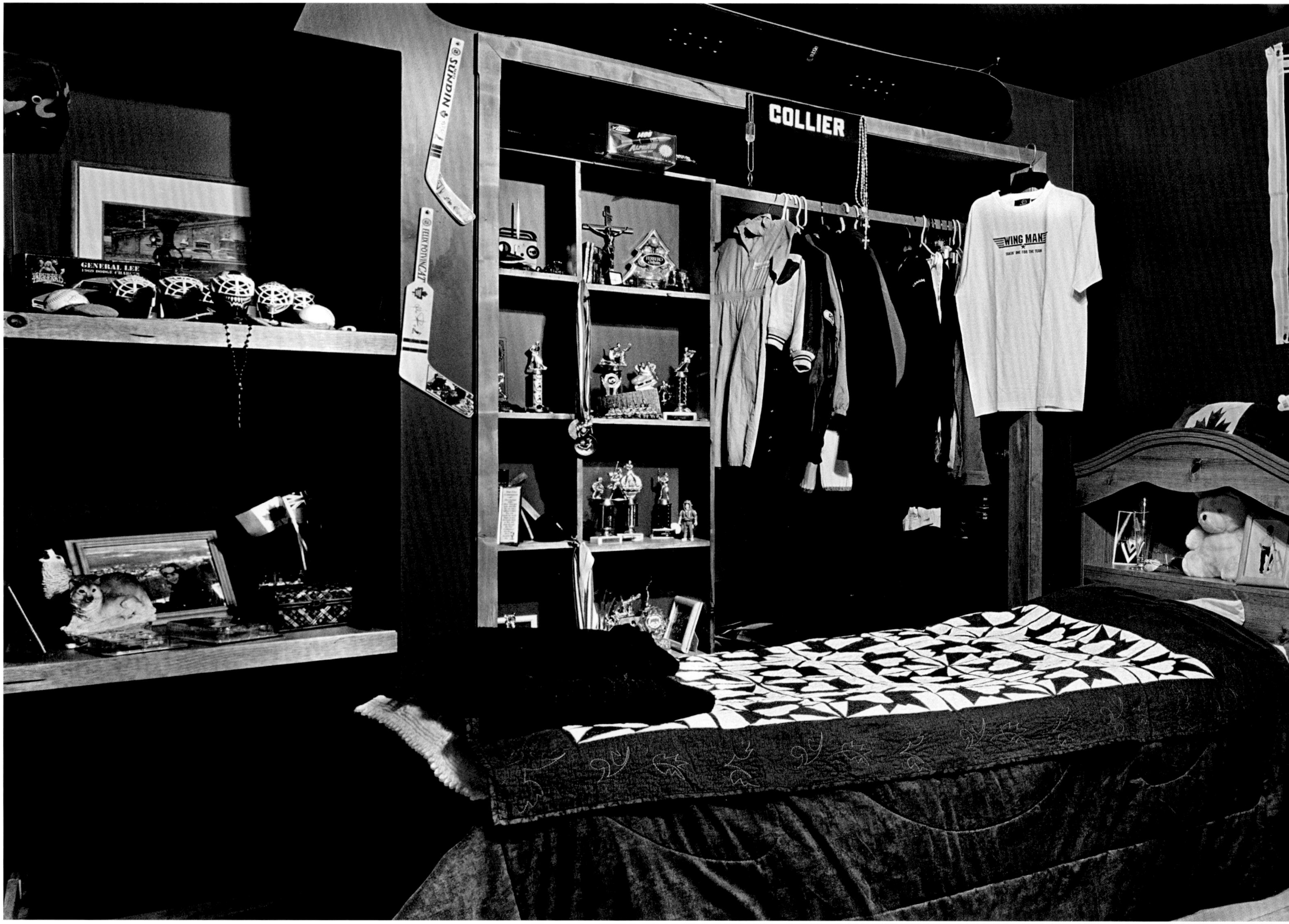
GENERAL LEE
SUNDIN
COLLIER
WING MAN

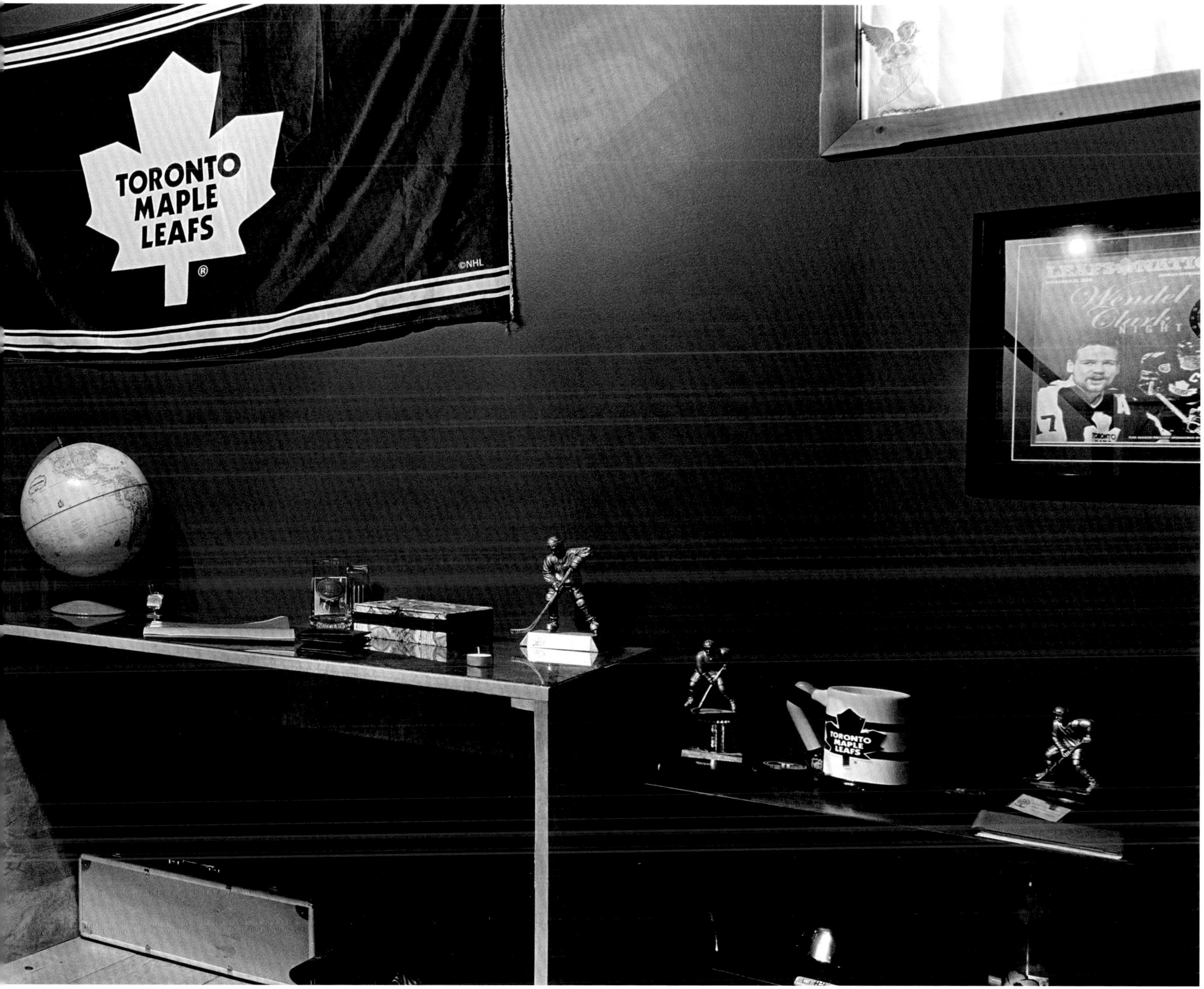

Sapper Brian Collier, 24, was killed by a roadside bomb on July 20, 2010, in the Panjwaii district, Afghanistan. He was from Bradford, Ontario, Canada. His bedroom was photographed in December 2010.

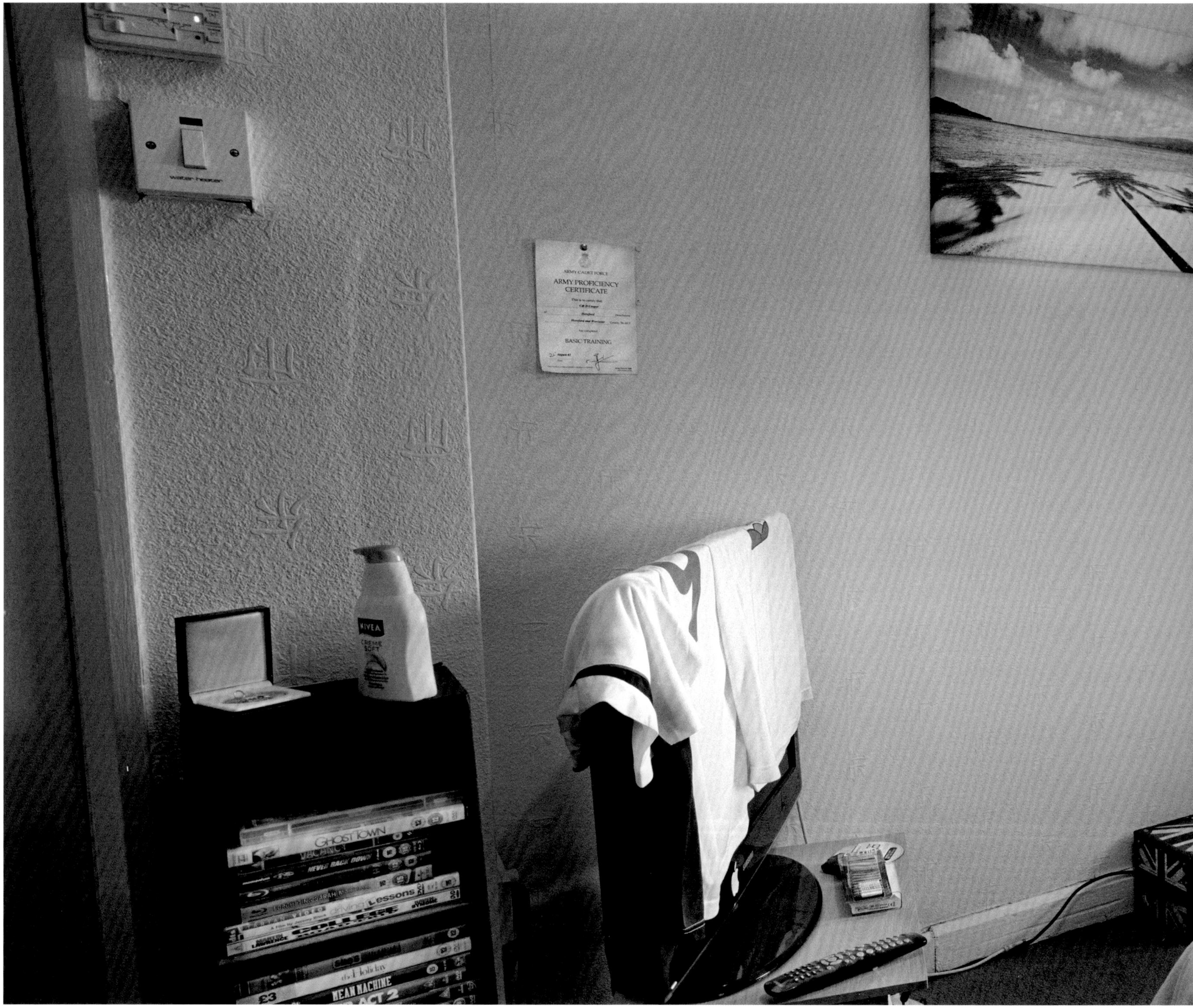

Lance Corporal Daniel Cooper, 21, was killed by a roadside bomb on January 24, 2010, in Helmand, Afghanistan. He was from Hereford, Herefordshire, England. His bedroom was photographed in March 2011.

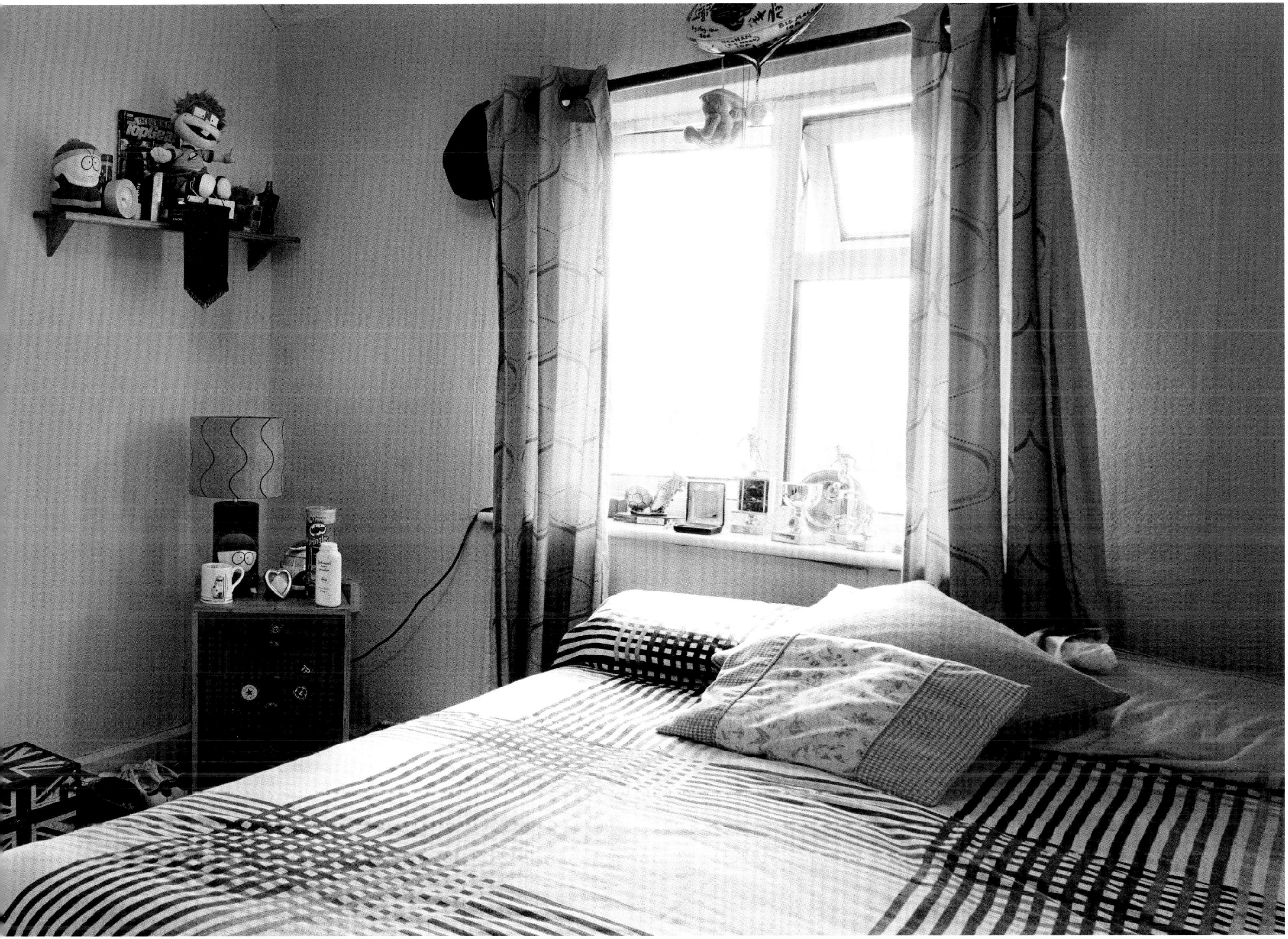

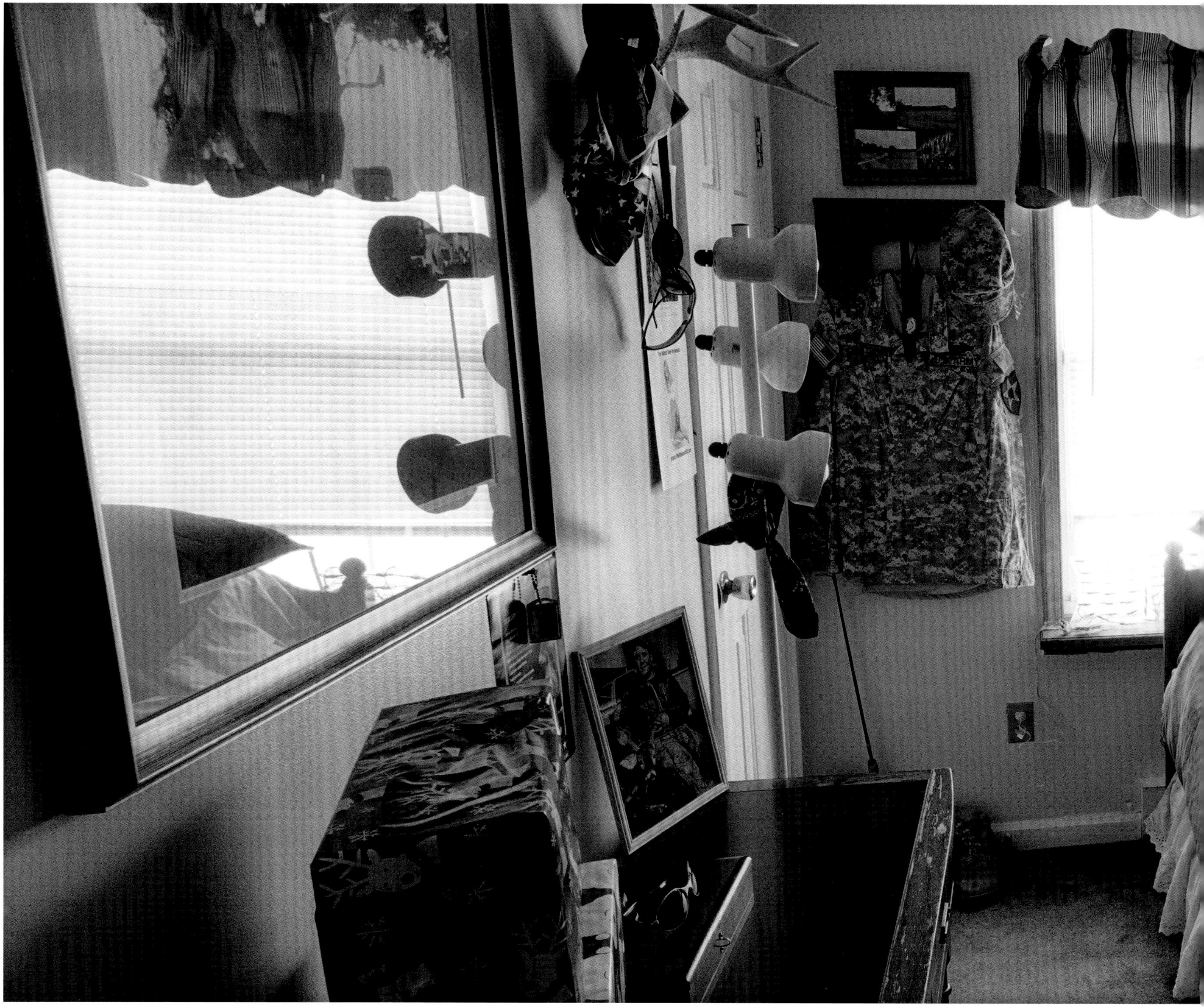

Army Corporal Brandon M. Craig, 25, was killed by a roadside bomb on July 19, 2007, in Husayniyah, Iraq. He was from Earleville, Maryland. His bedroom was photographed in February 2010.

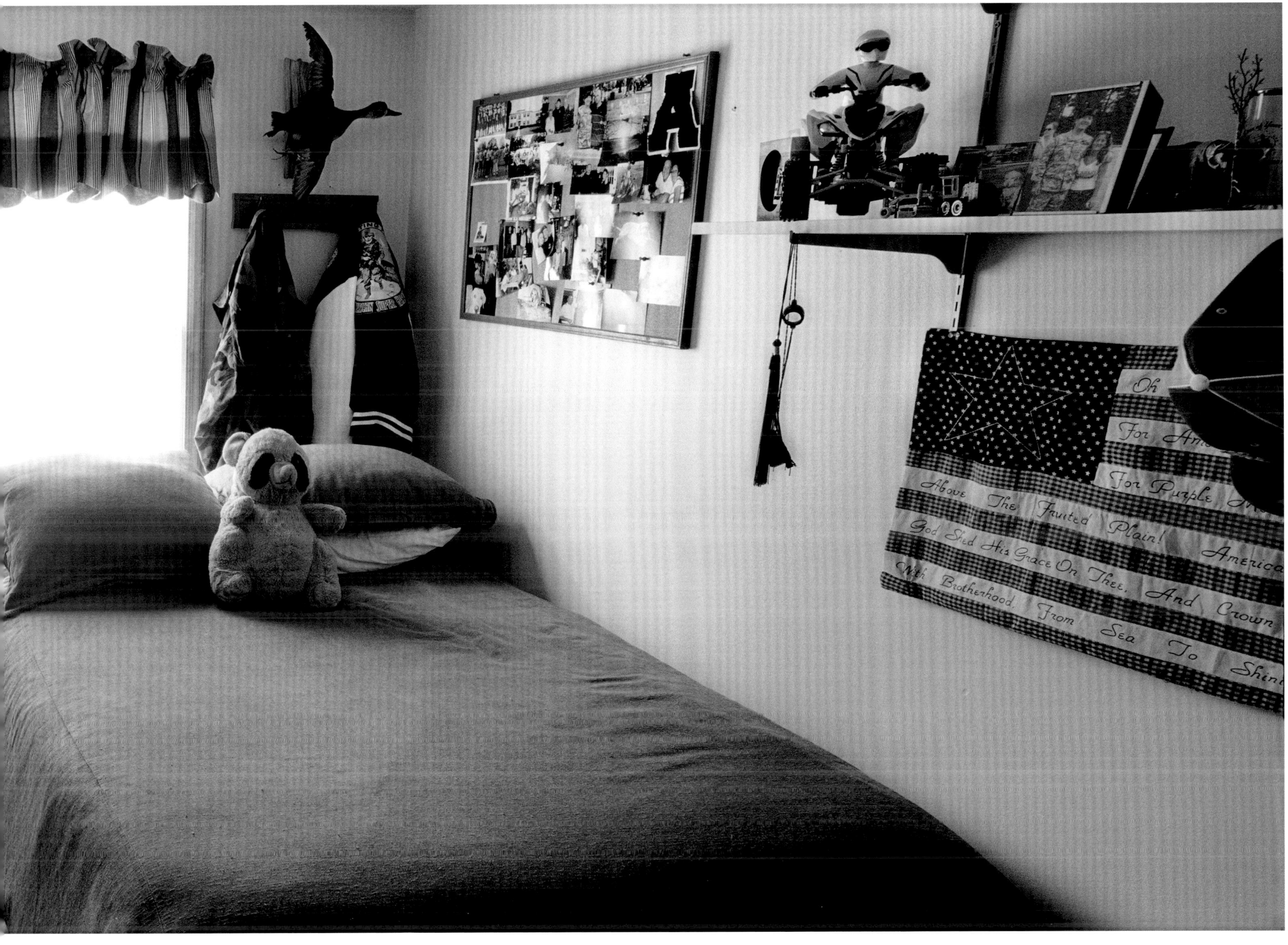
Oh
For Purple
Above The Fruited Plain!
America
God Shed His Grace On Thee.
And Crown
With Brotherhood. From Sea To

Rifleman Paul Donnachie, 18, was killed by small arms fire on April 24, 2007, in Basra, Iraq. He was from Reading, England. His bedroom was photographed in March 2011.

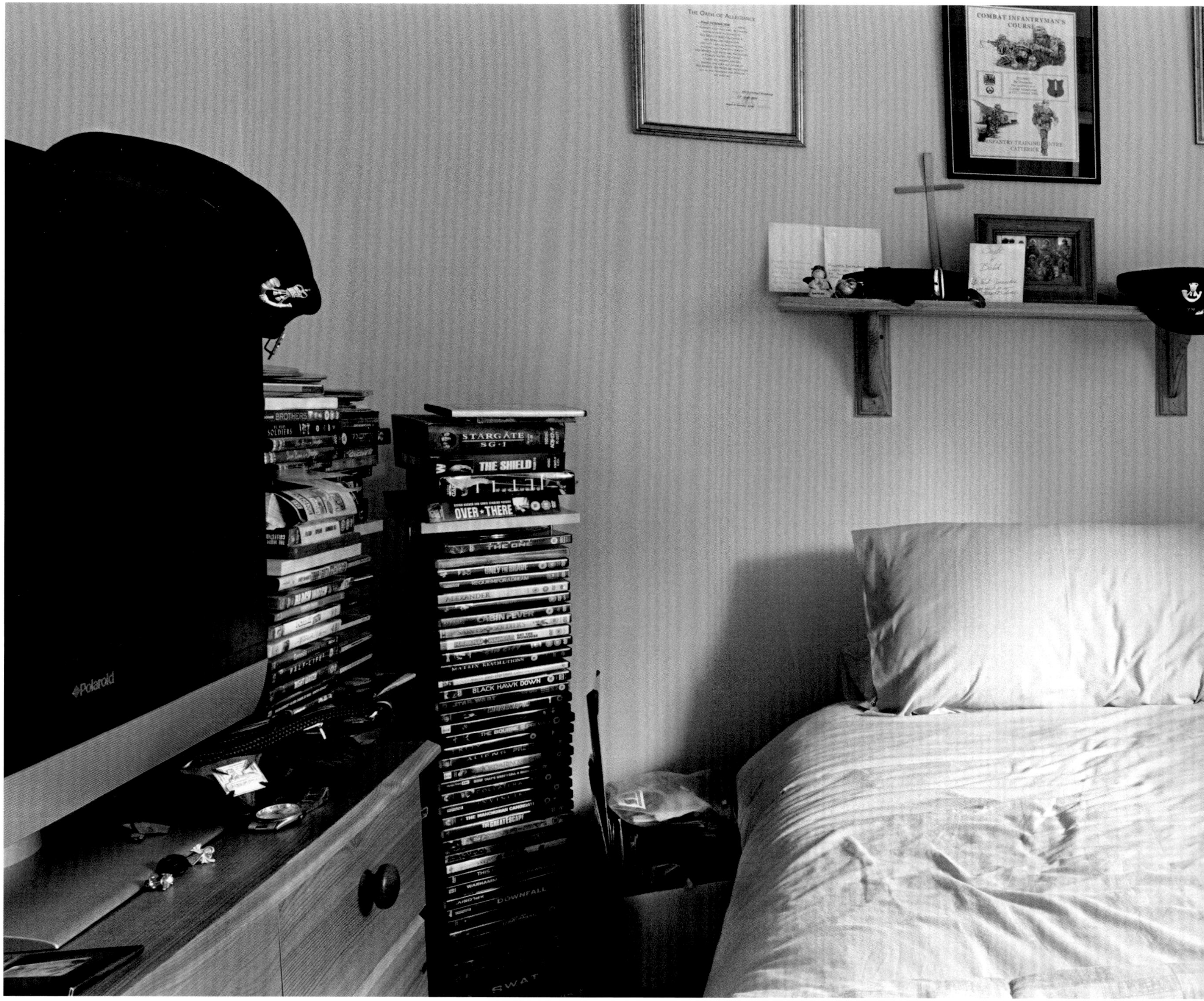

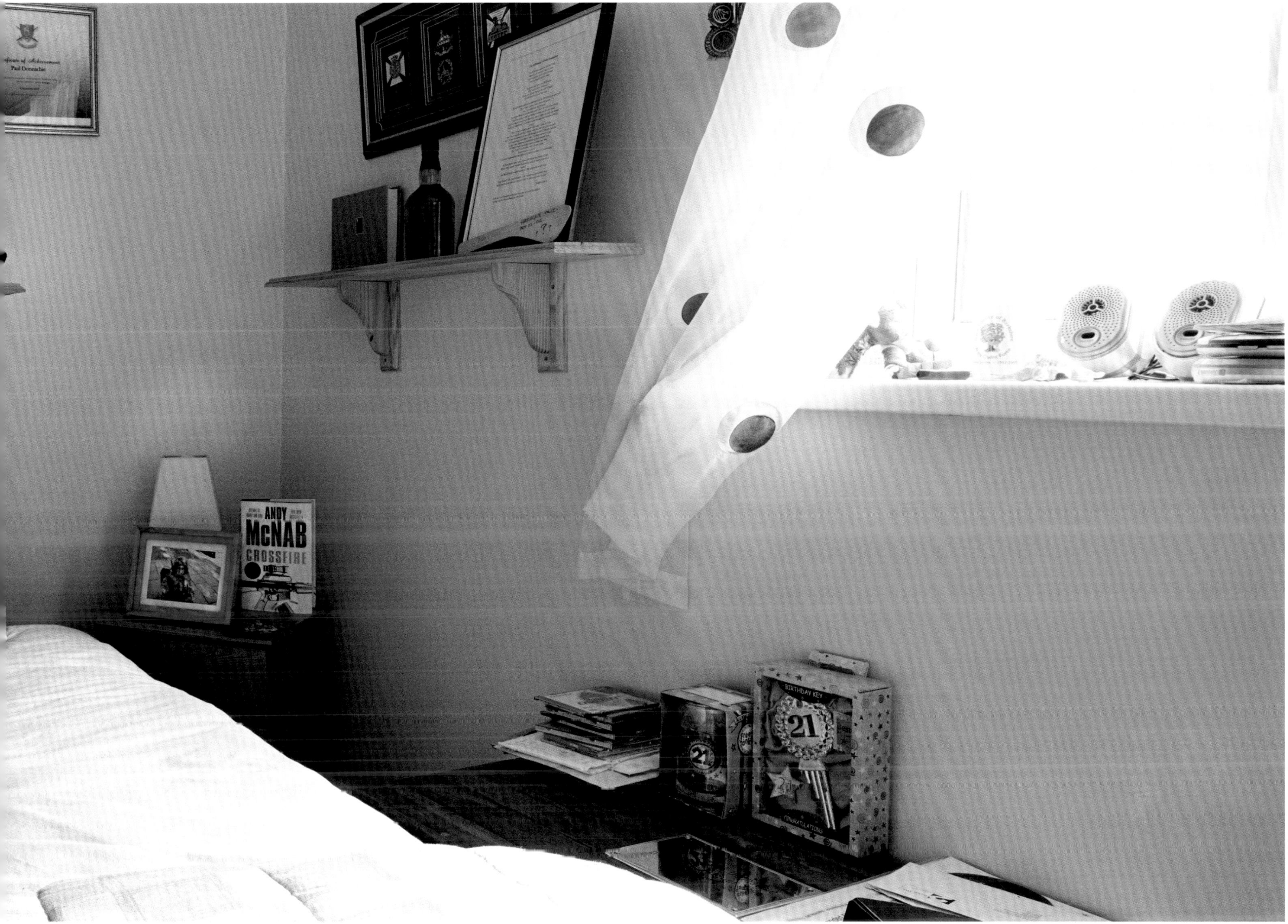
ANDY
McNAB
CROSSFIRE
BIRTHDAY KEY
21

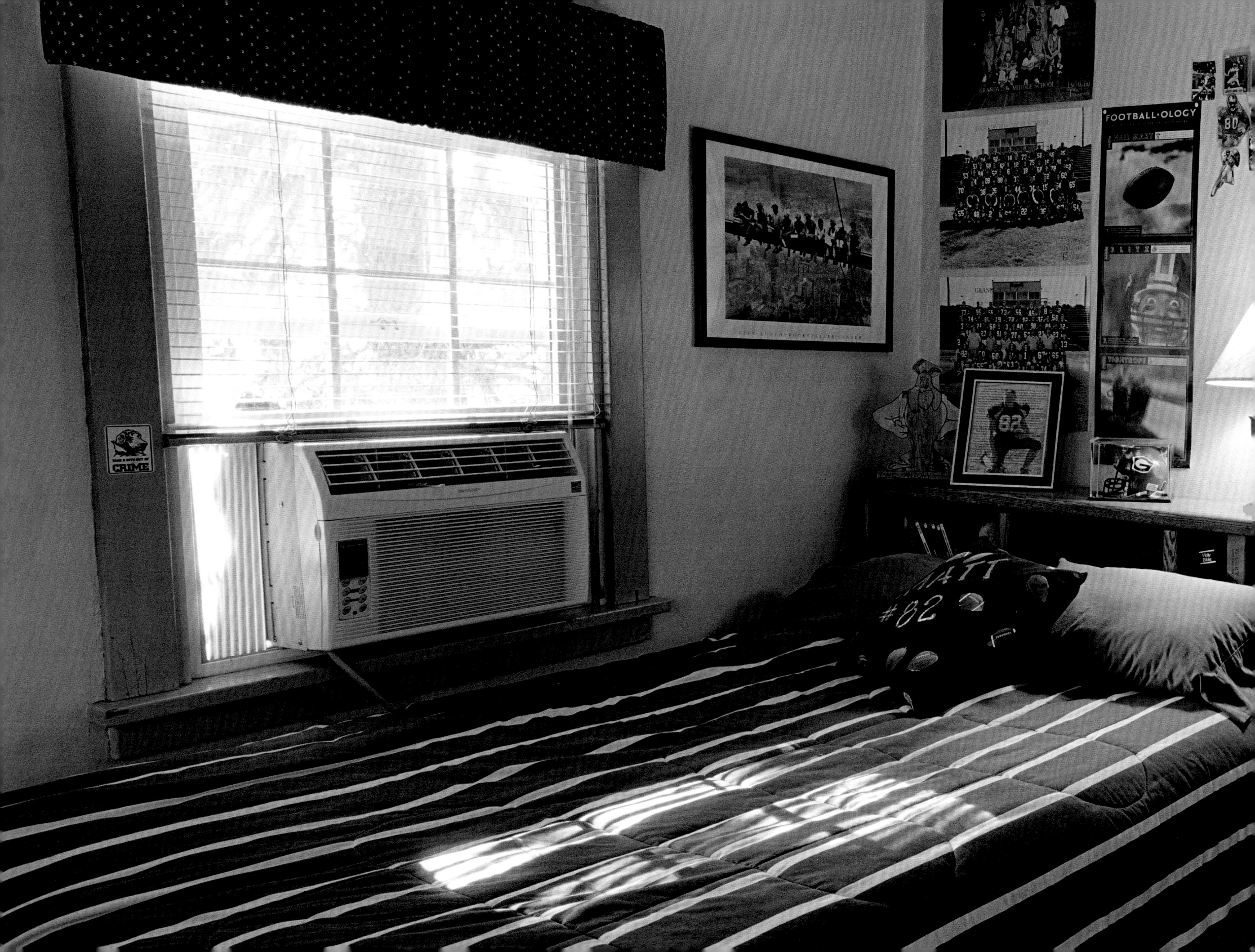
FOOTBALL·OLOGY
CRIME
#82

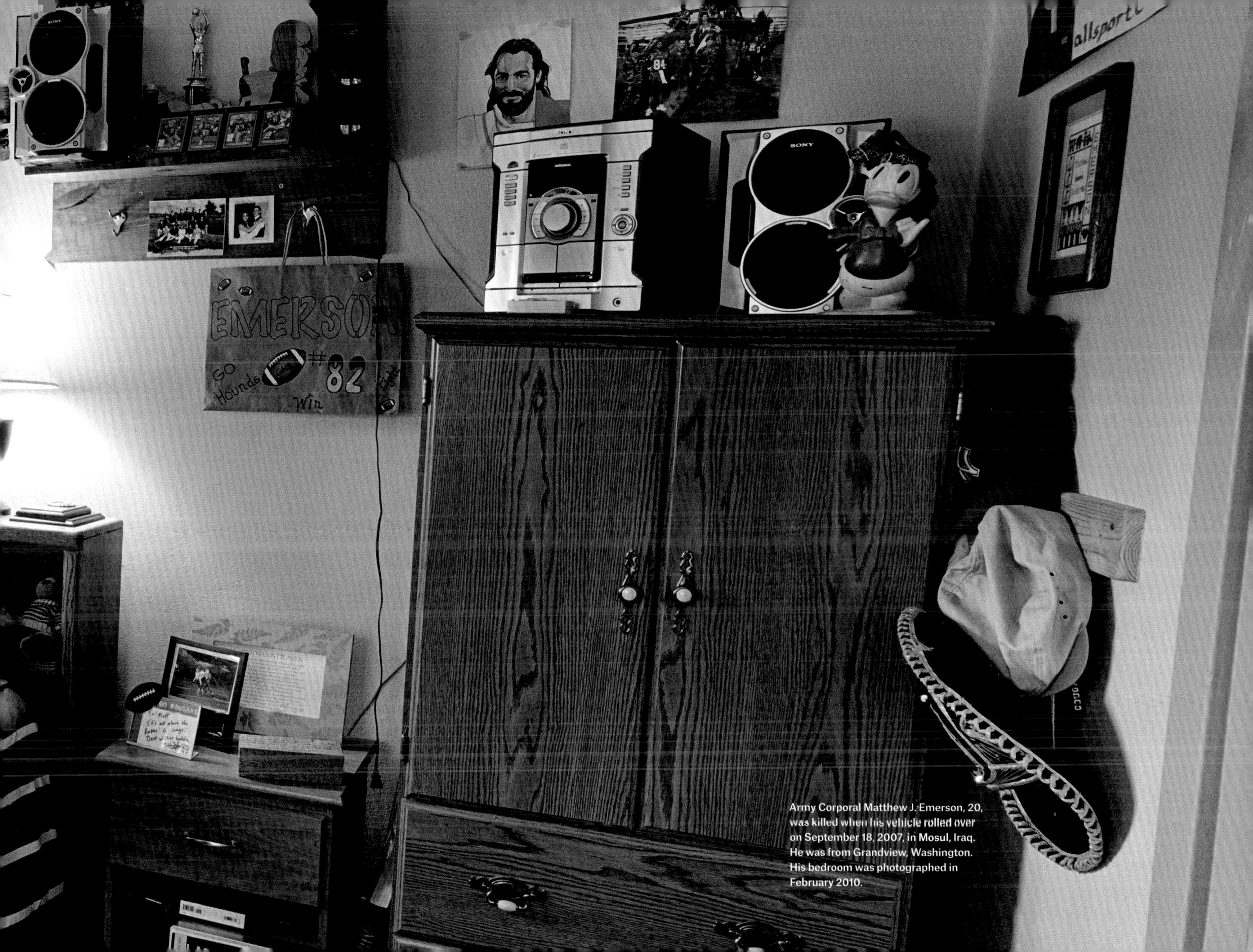

Army Corporal Matthew J. Emerson, 20, was killed when his vehicle rolled over on September 18, 2007, in Mosul, Iraq. He was from Grandview, Washington. His bedroom was photographed in February 2010.

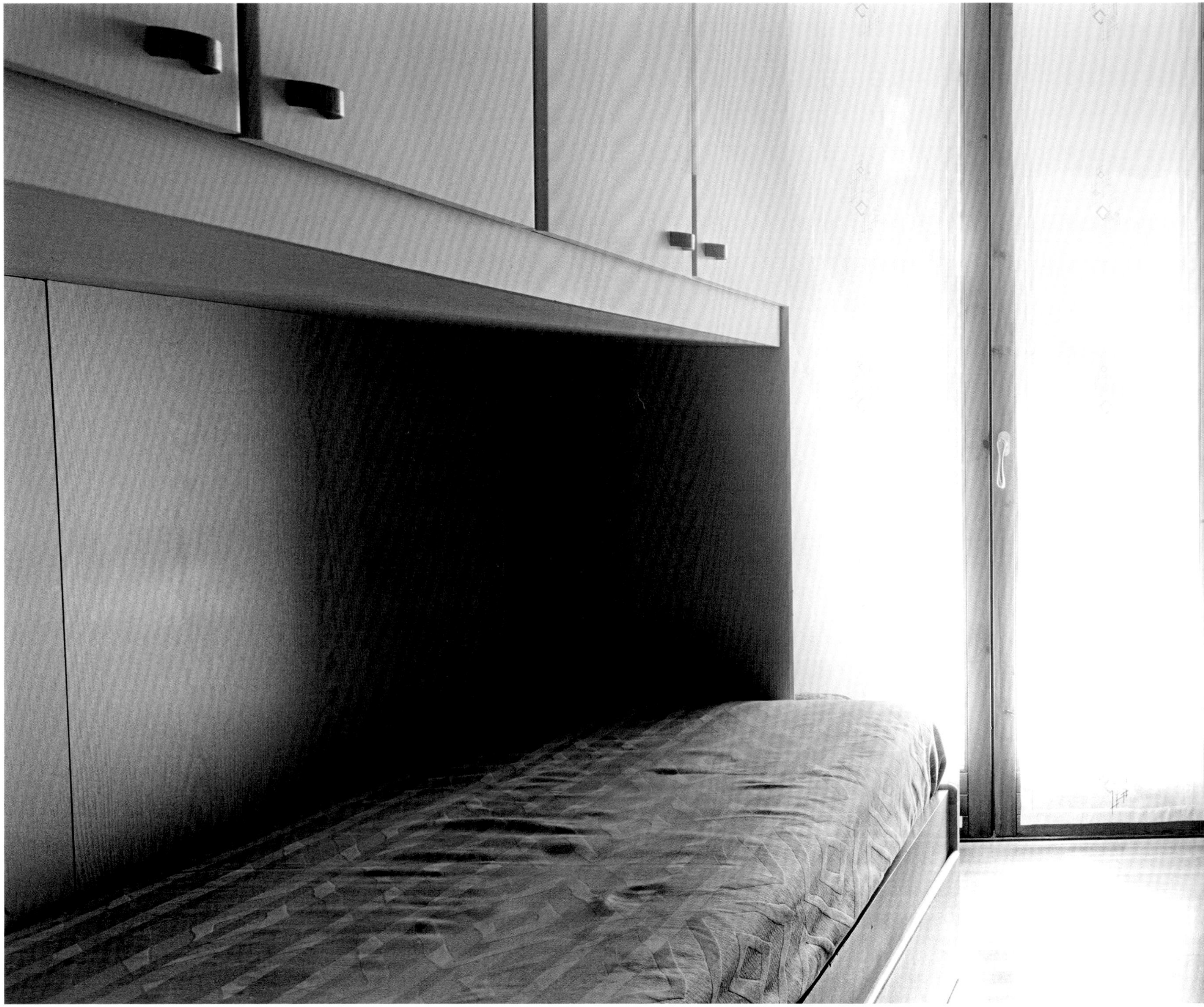

Captain Manuel Fiorito, 27, was killed by a roadside bomb on May 5, 2006, in the Musa Valley, Afghanistan. He was from Verona, Veneto, Italy. His bedroom was photographed in August 2011.

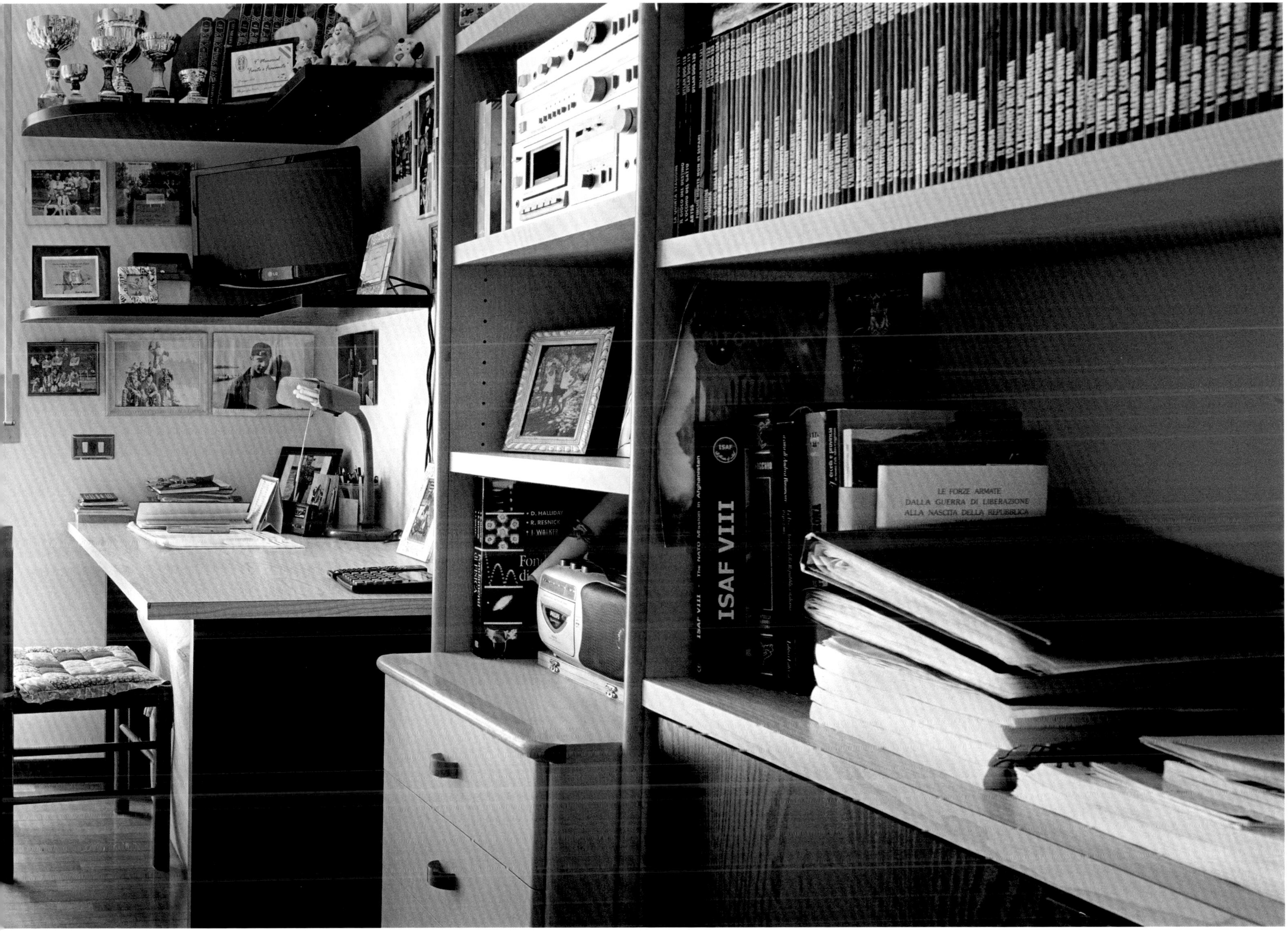
D. HALLIDAY
R. RESNICK
ISAF VIII
LE FORZE ARMATE
DALLA GUERRA DI LIBERAZIONE
ALLA NASCITA DELLA REPUBBLICA

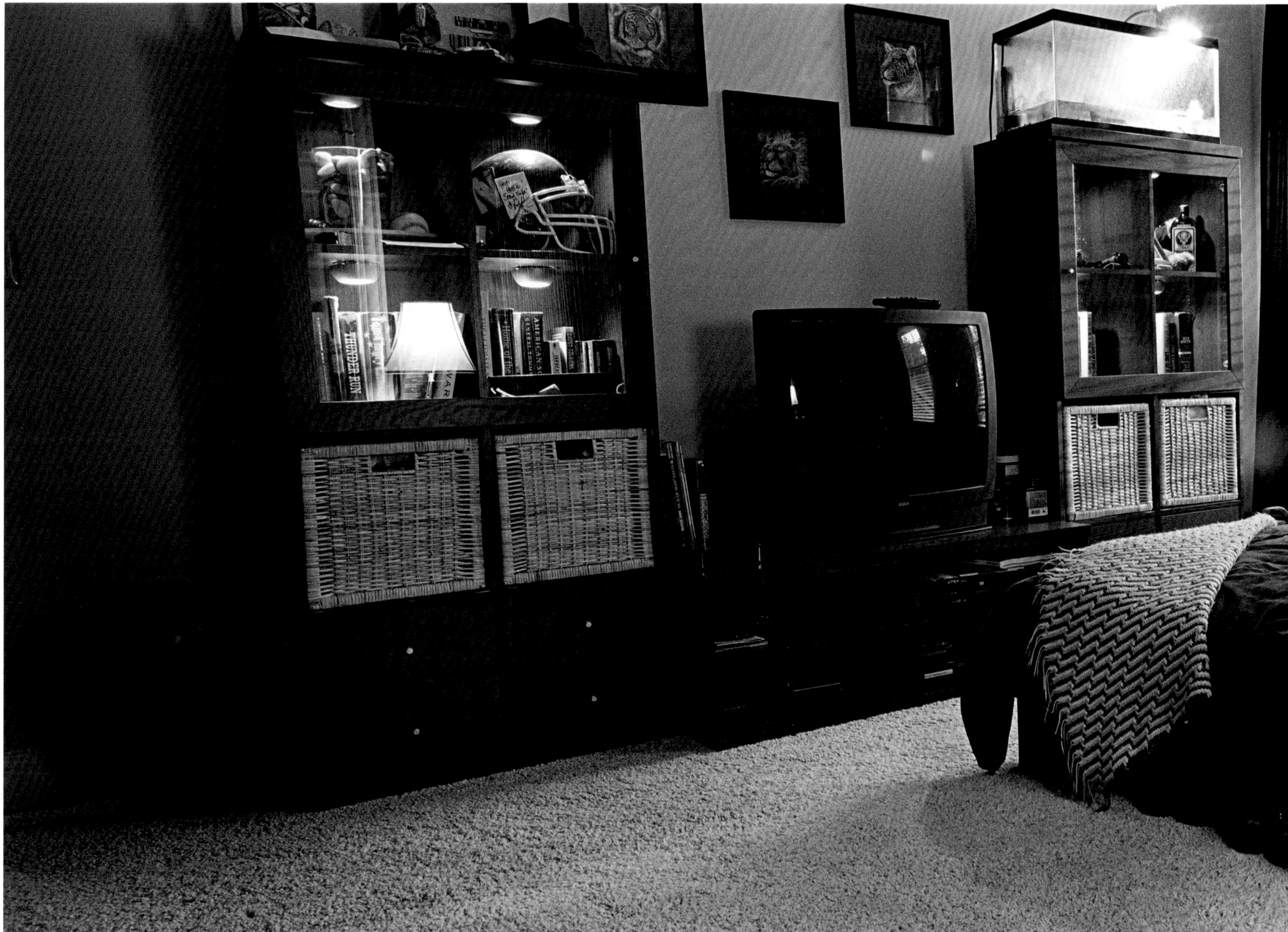
THUNDER RUN

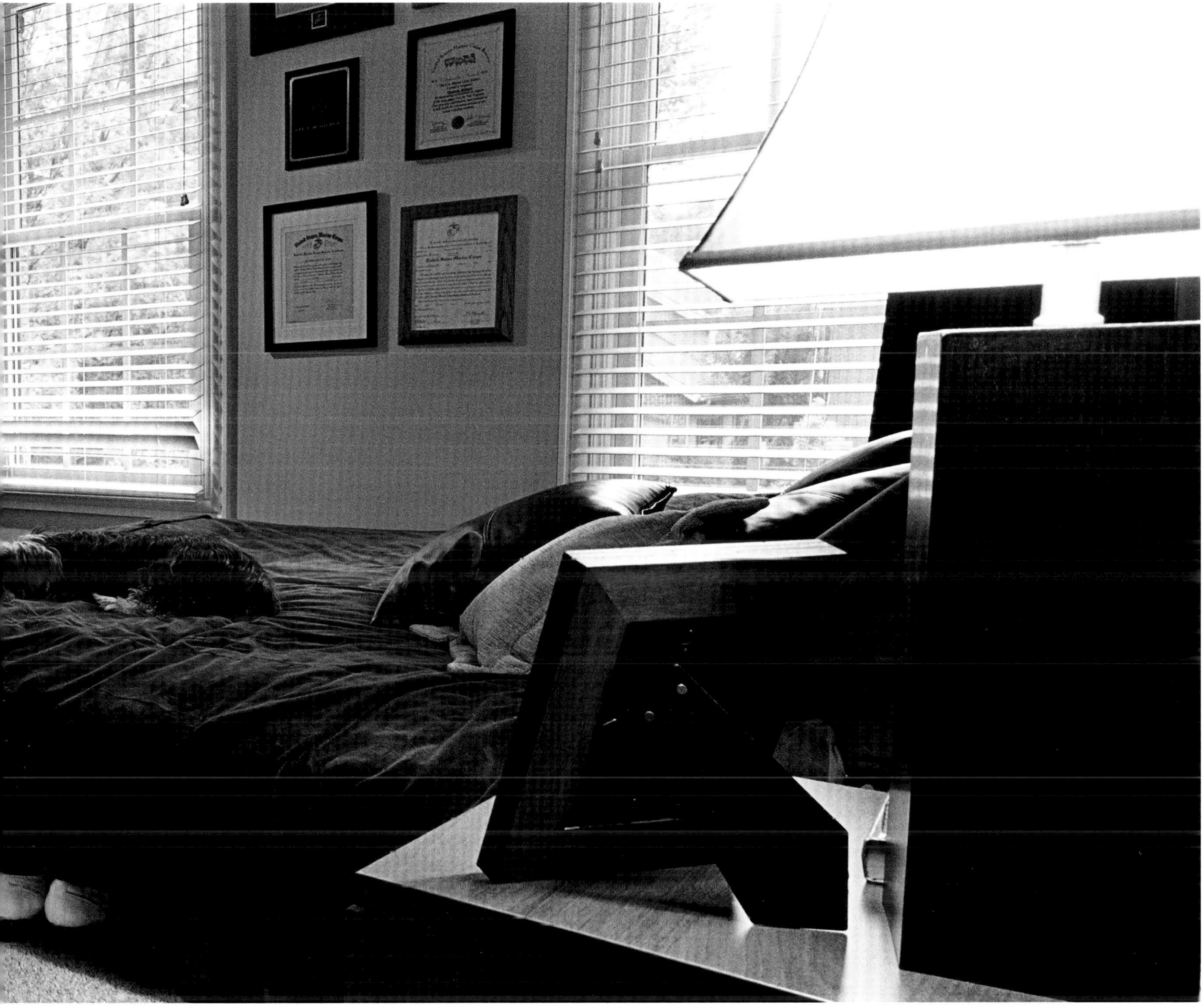

Marine Sergeant Thomas M. Gilbert, 24, was killed by a roadside bomb on October 25, 2006, in Falluja, Iraq. He was from Downers Grove, Illinois. His bedroom was photographed in July 2007.

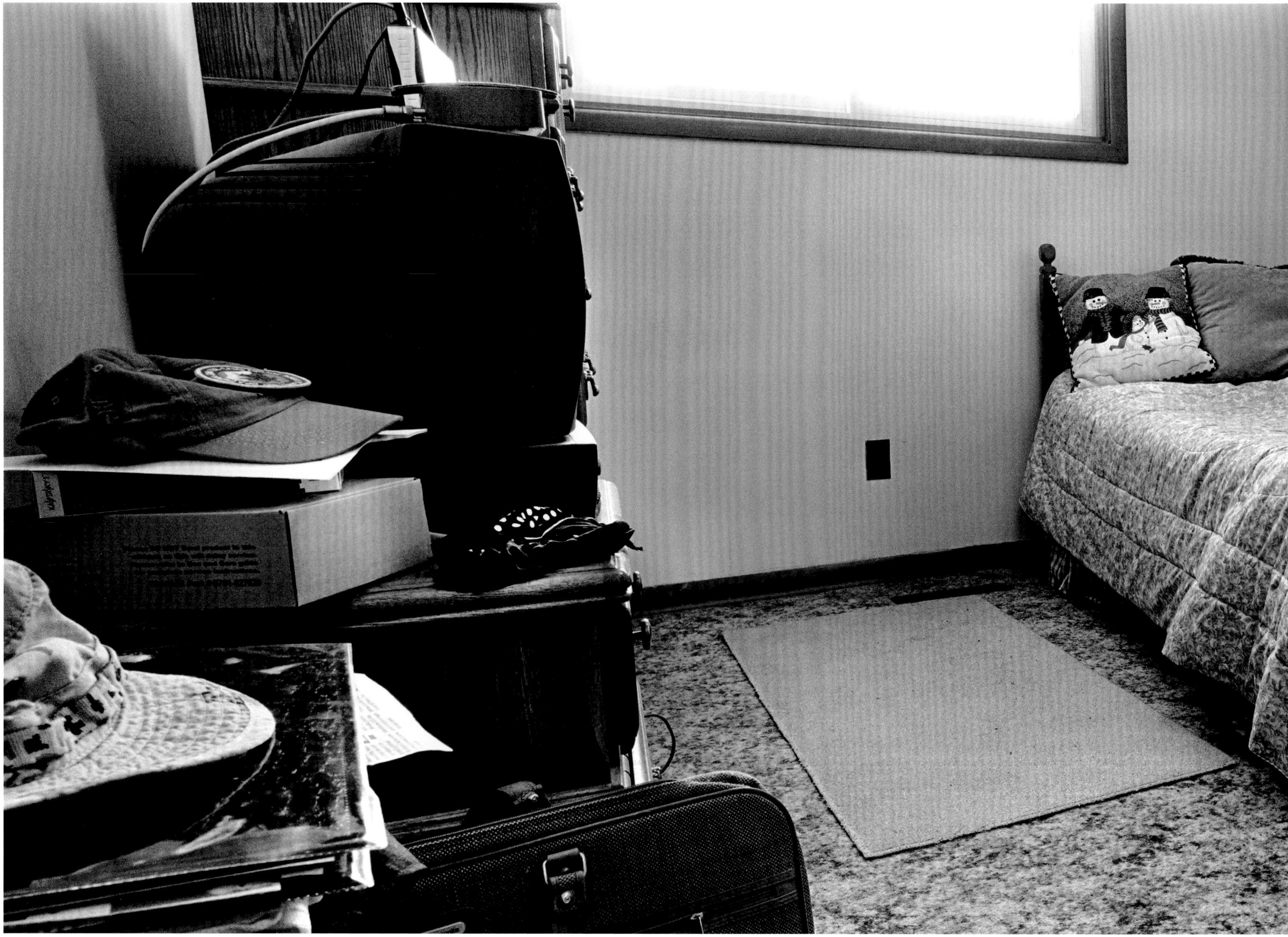

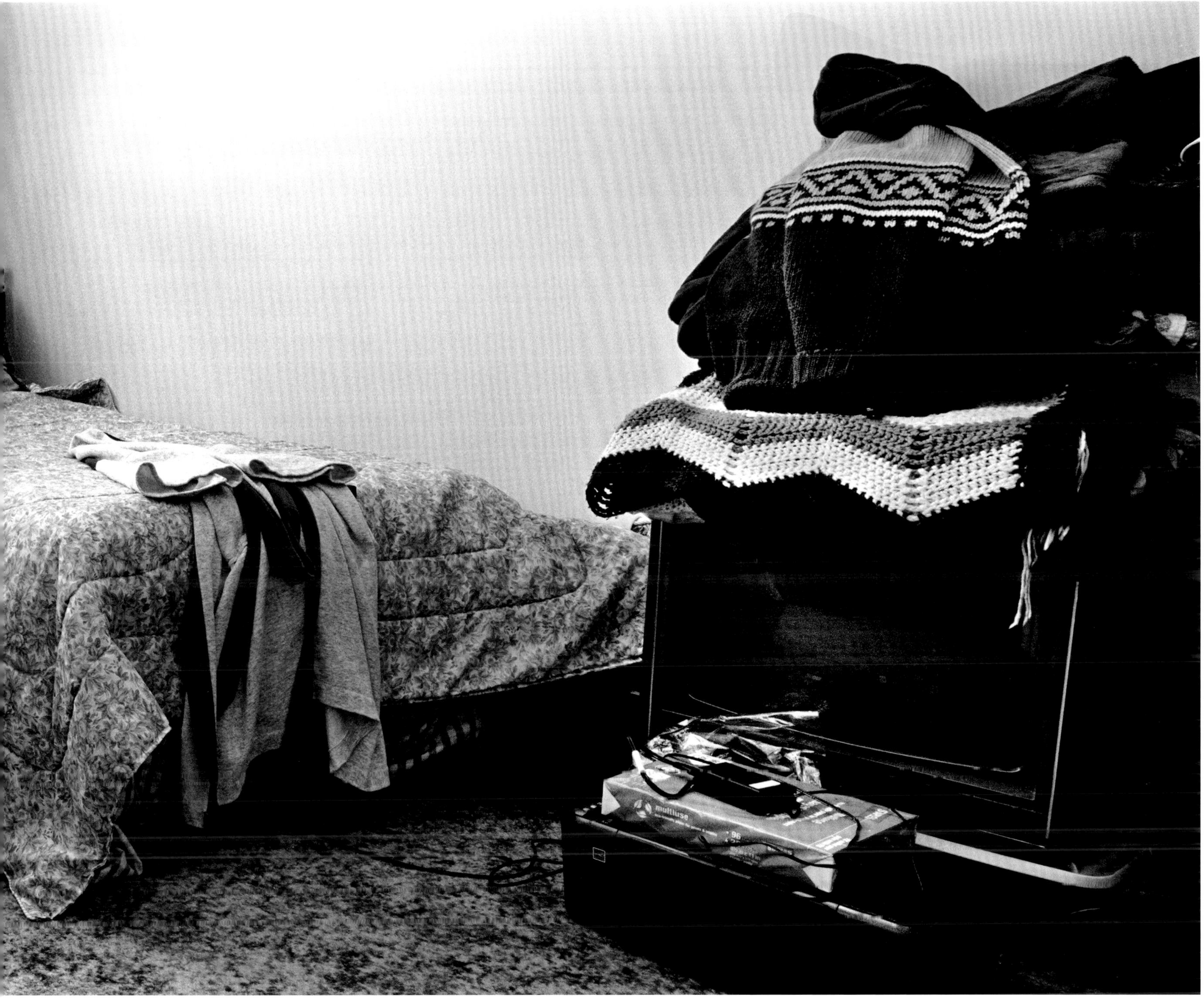

Corporal Andrew Grenon, 23, was killed when insurgents attacked his vehicle on September 3, 2008, in Kandahar, Afghanistan. He was from Windsor, Ontario, Canada. His bedroom was photographed in December 2010.

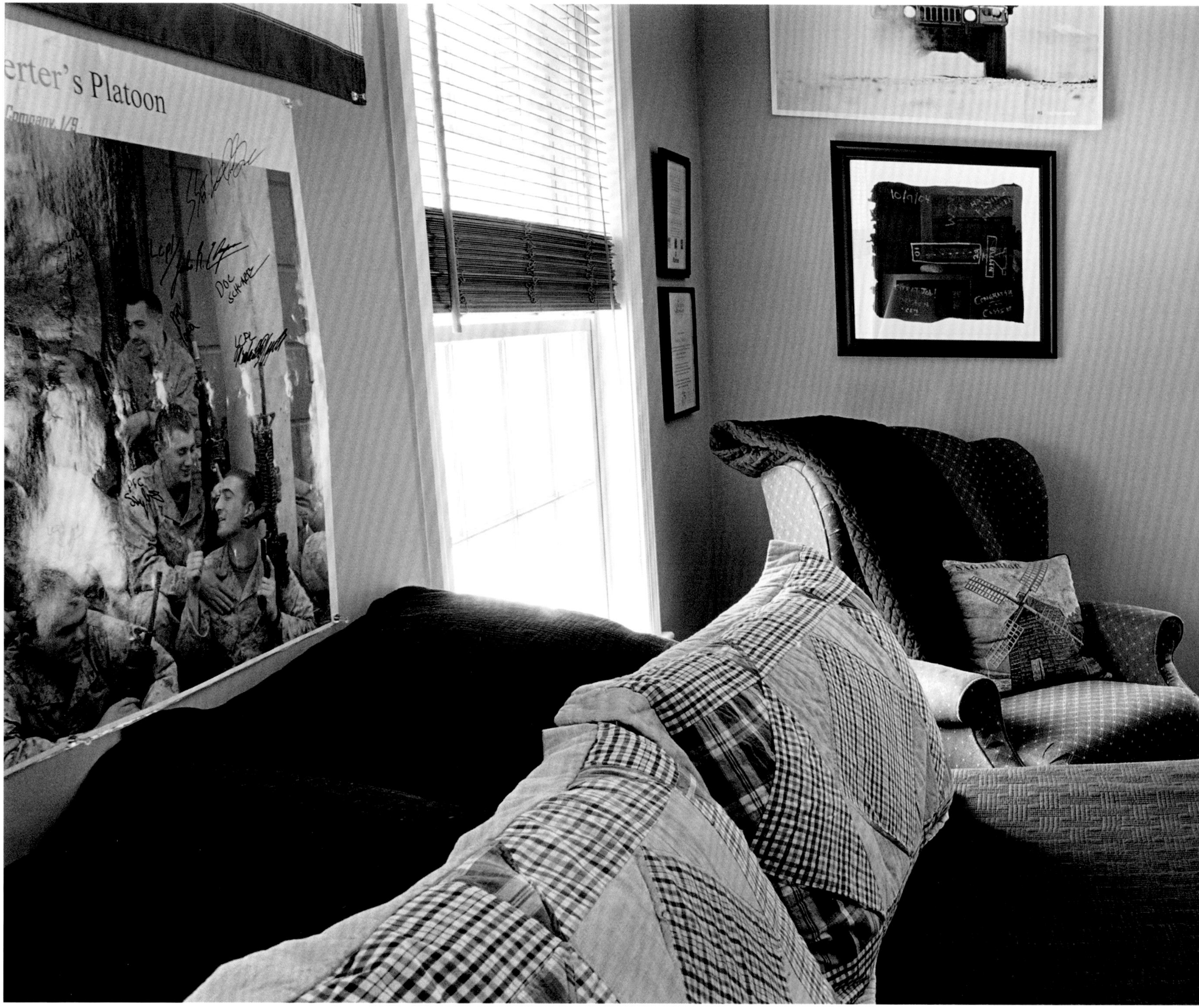

Marine Lance Corporal Jordan C. Haerter, 19, was killed by a suicide truck bomb on April 22, 2008, in Ramadi, Iraq. He was from Sag Harbor, New York. His bedroom was photographed in January 2010.

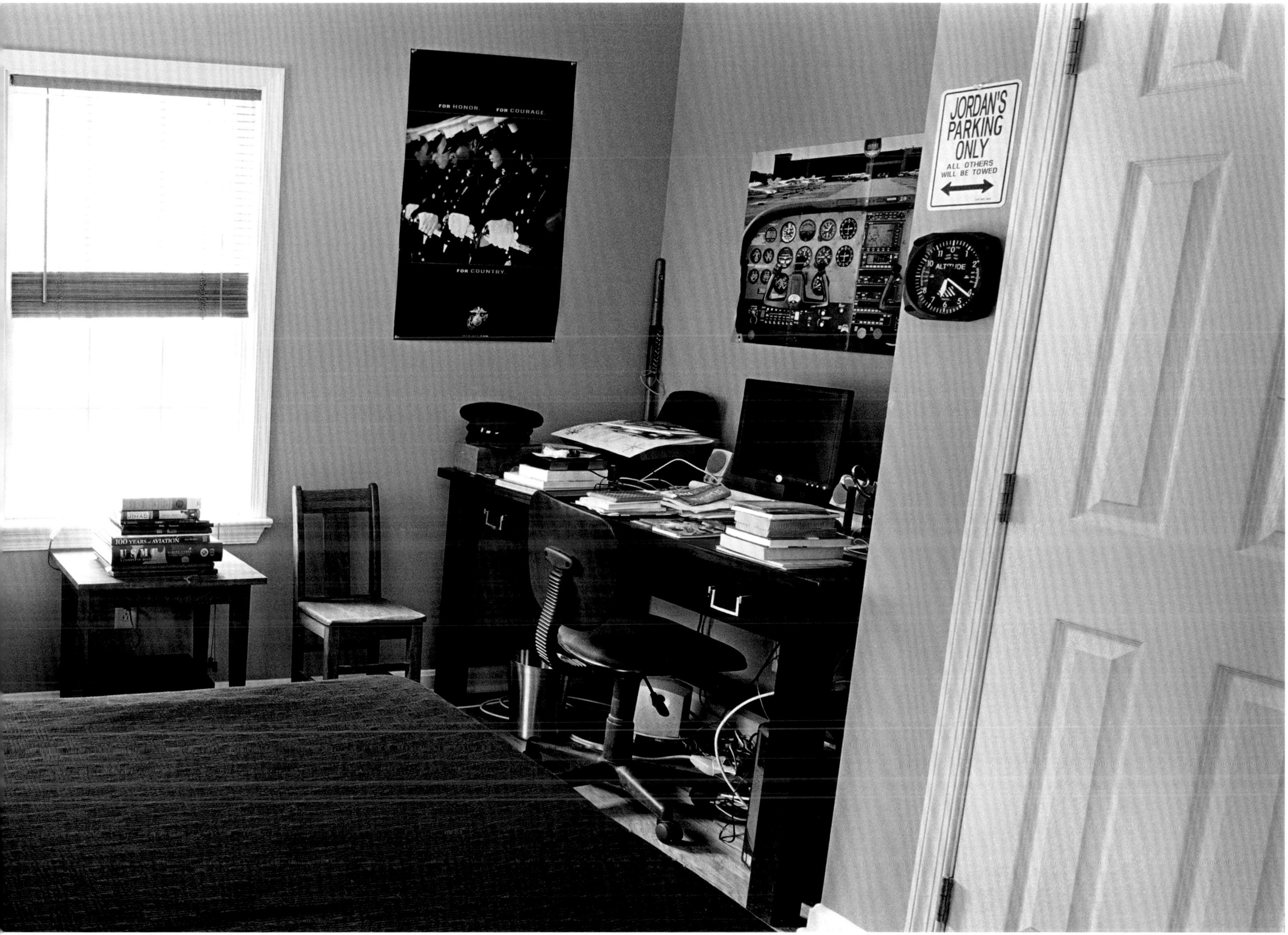
FOR HONOR.
FOR COURAGE.
FOR COUNTRY.
JORDAN'S PARKING ONLY
ALL OTHERS WILL BE TOWED
ALTITUDE
100 YEARS of AVIATION
USMC

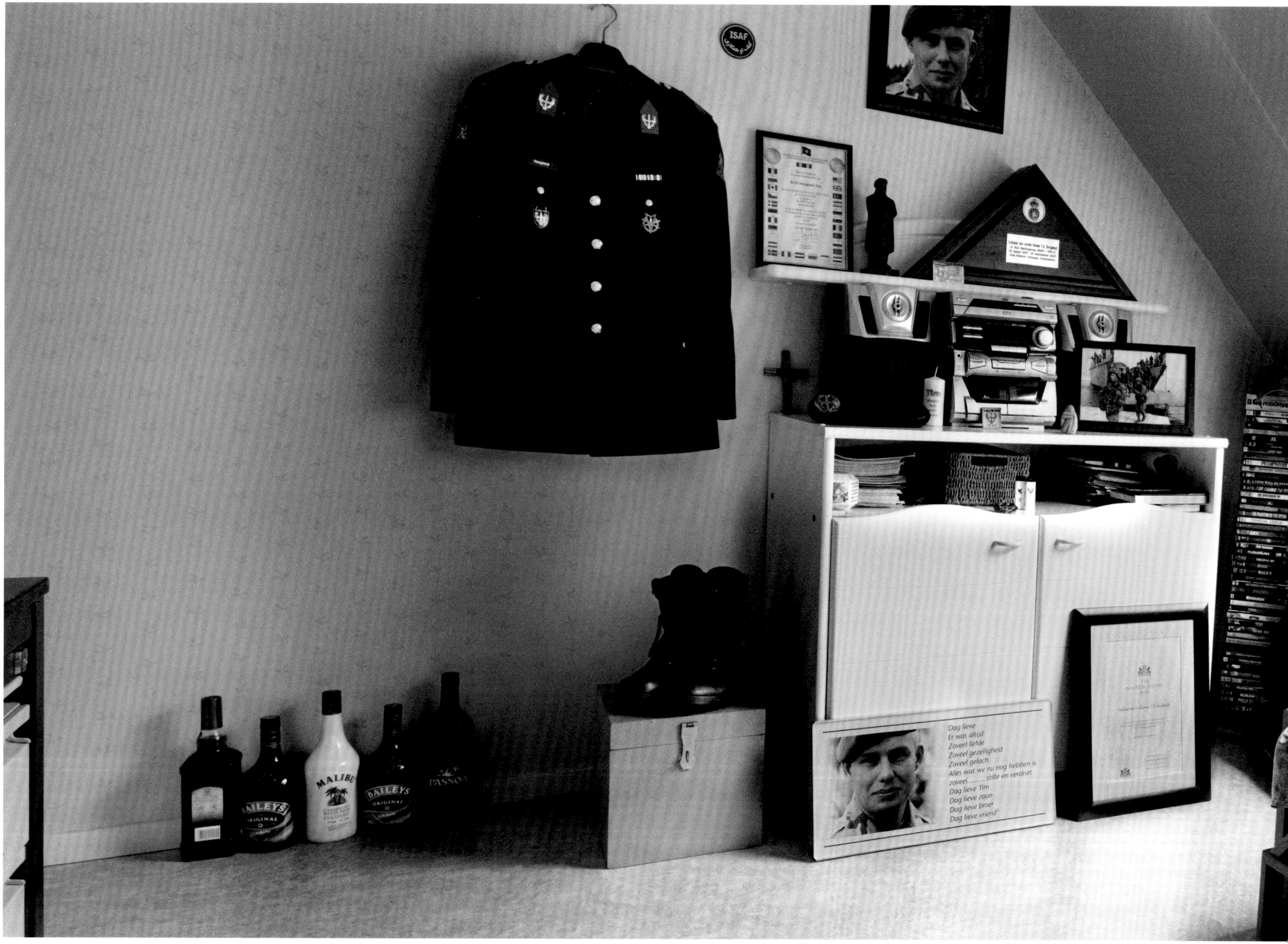
ISAF
BAILEYS
ORIGINAL
MALIBU
BAILEYS
ORIGINAL
'Dag lieve
Er was altijd:
Zoveel liefde
Zoveel gezelligheid
Zoveel gelach.
Alles wat we nu nog hebben is
zoveel..........stilte en verdriet
Dag lieve Tim
Dag lieve zoon
Dag lieve broer
Dag lieve vriend'

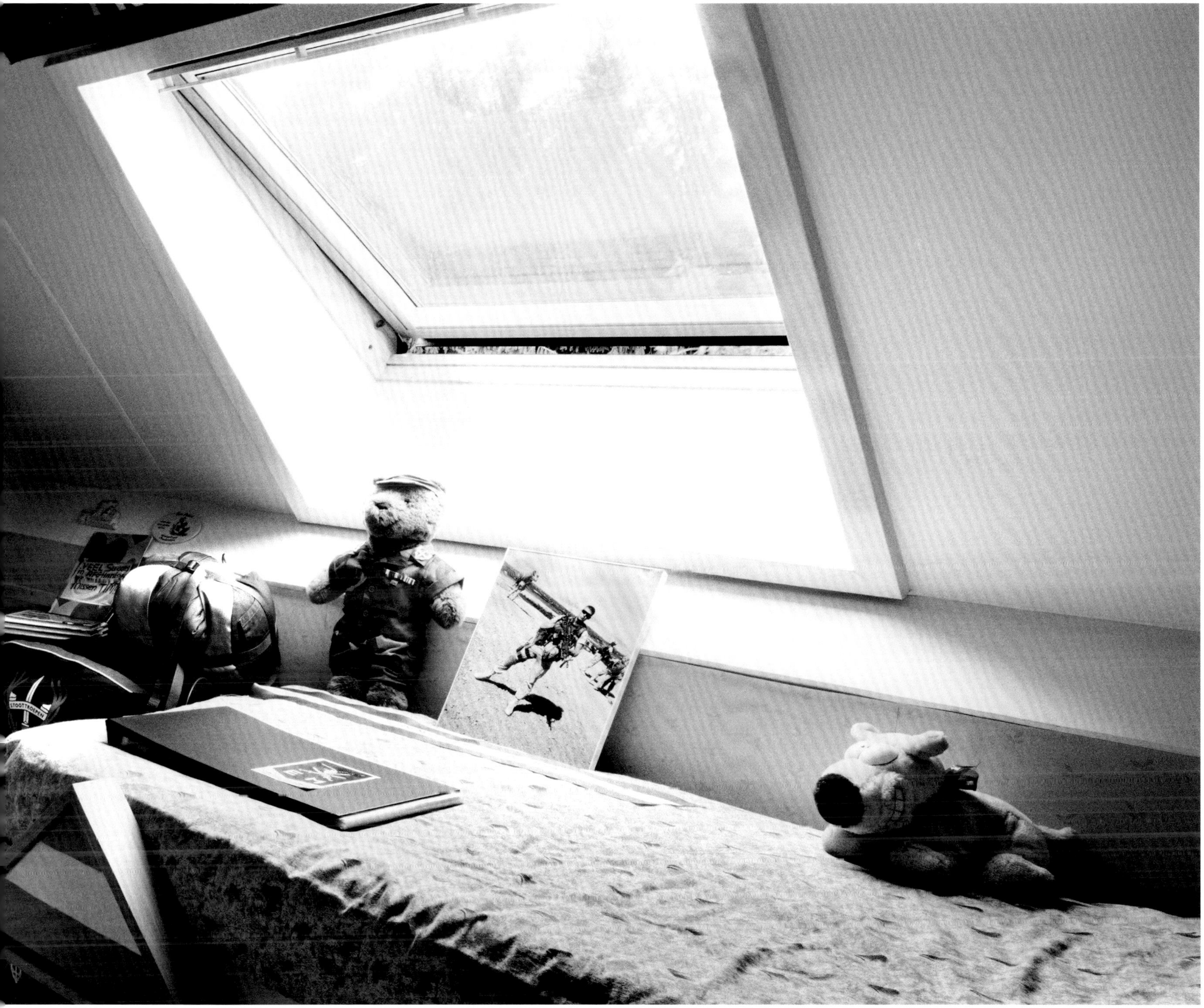

Soldier First Class Tim Hoogland, 20, was killed in an ambush on September 20, 2007, in Deh Rawod, Afghanistan. He was from Vroomshoop, Overijissel, The Netherlands. His bedroom was photographed in October 2010.

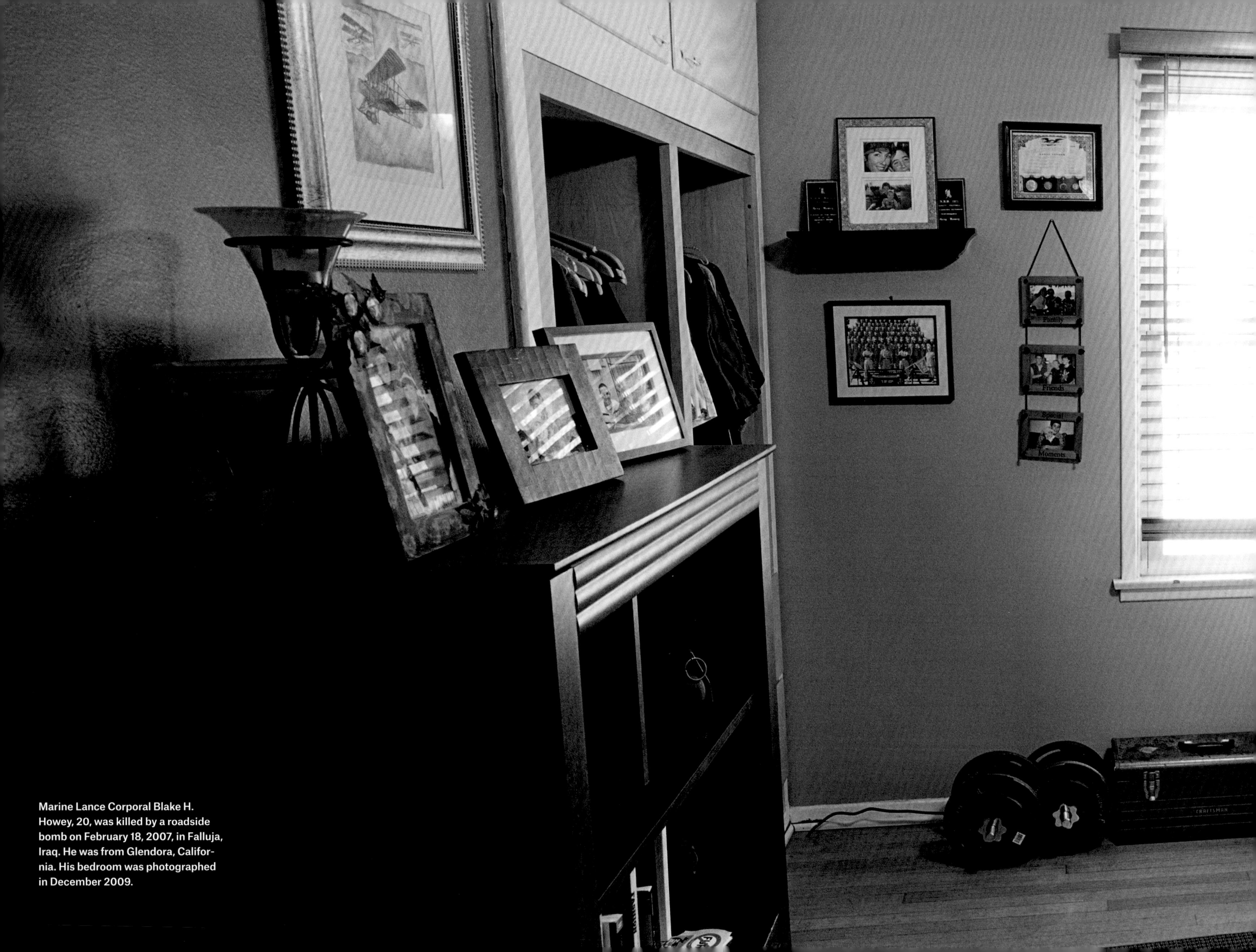

Marine Lance Corporal Blake H. Howey, 20, was killed by a roadside bomb on February 18, 2007, in Falluja, Iraq. He was from Glendora, California. His bedroom was photographed in December 2009.

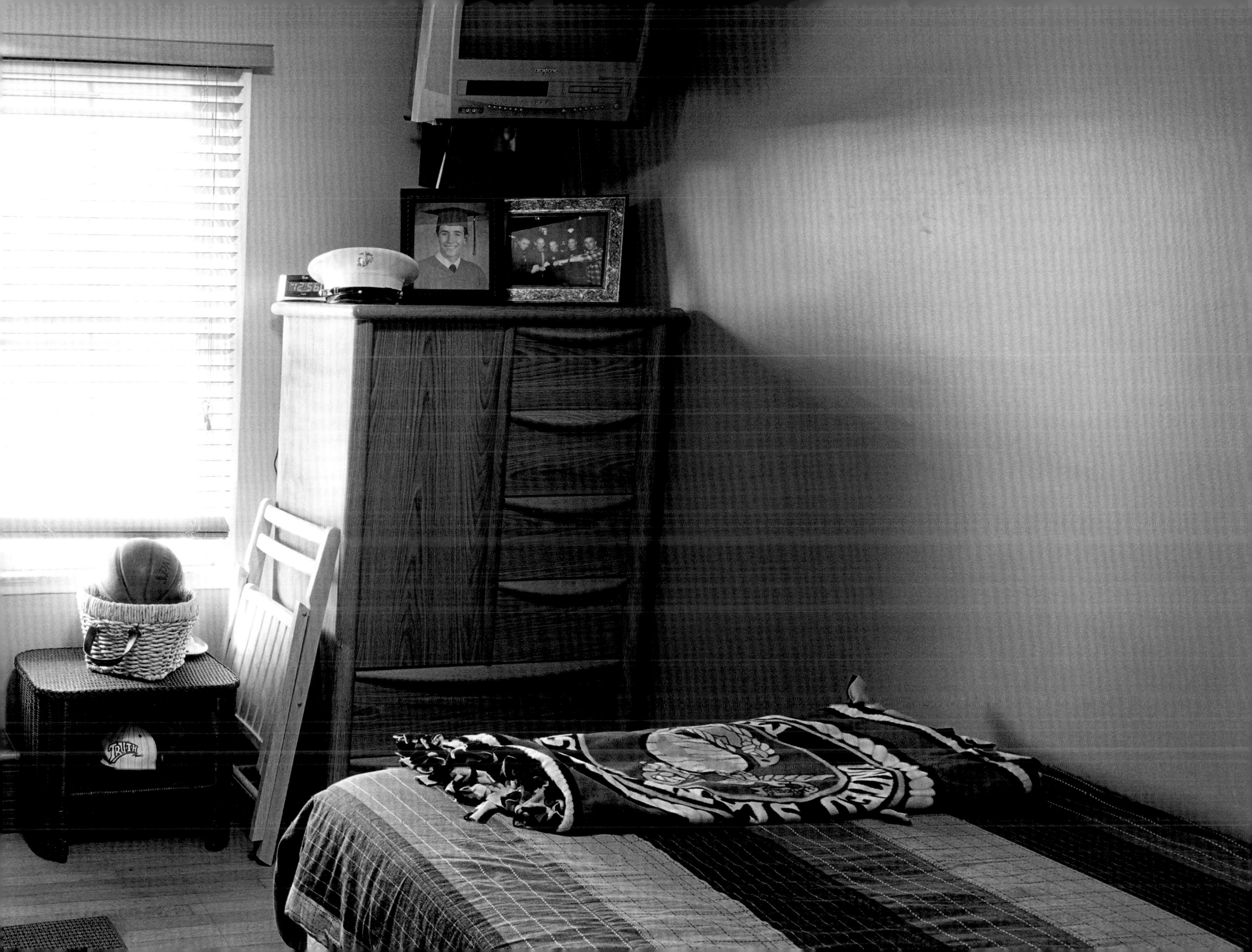

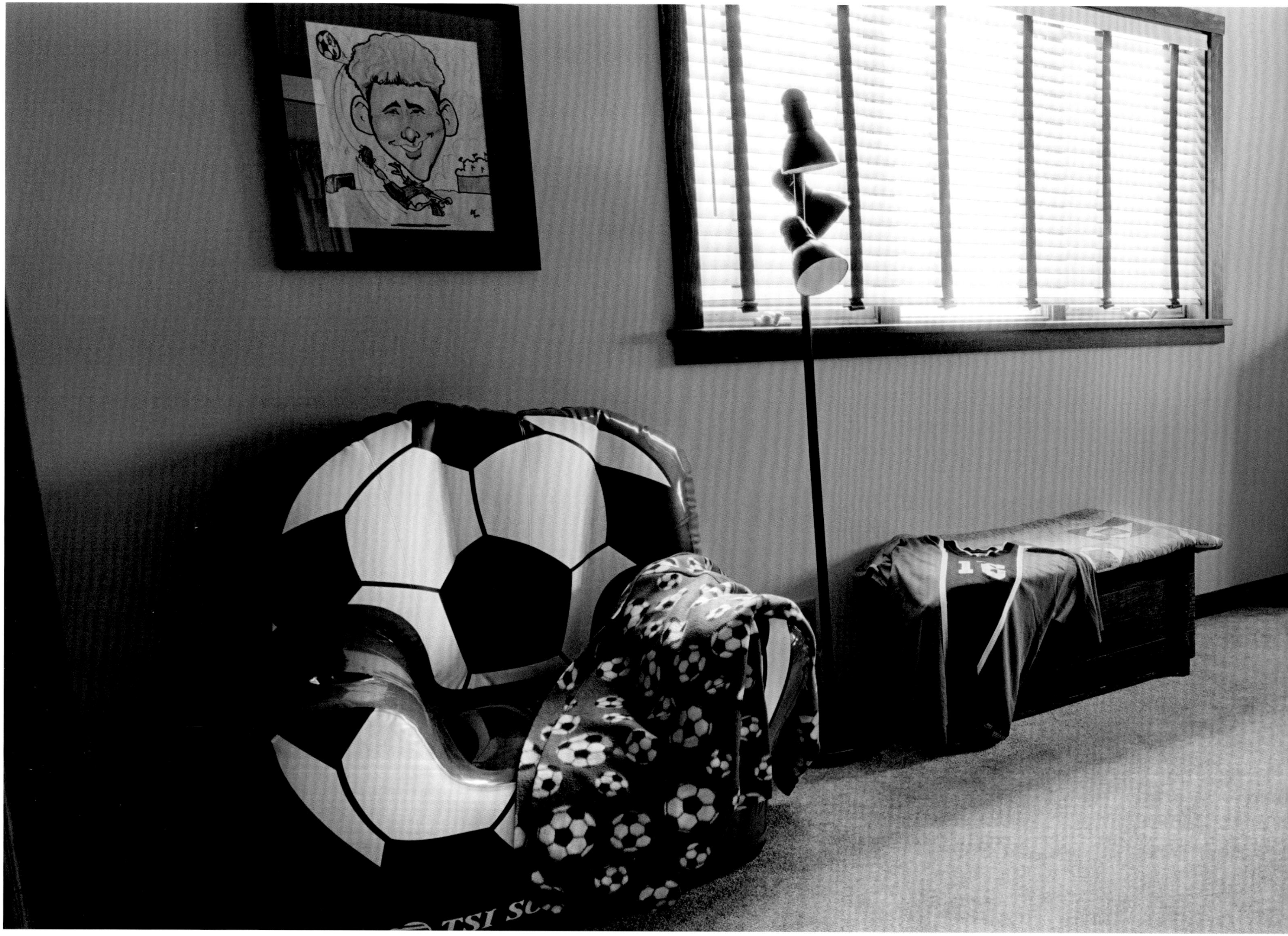
16
TSI

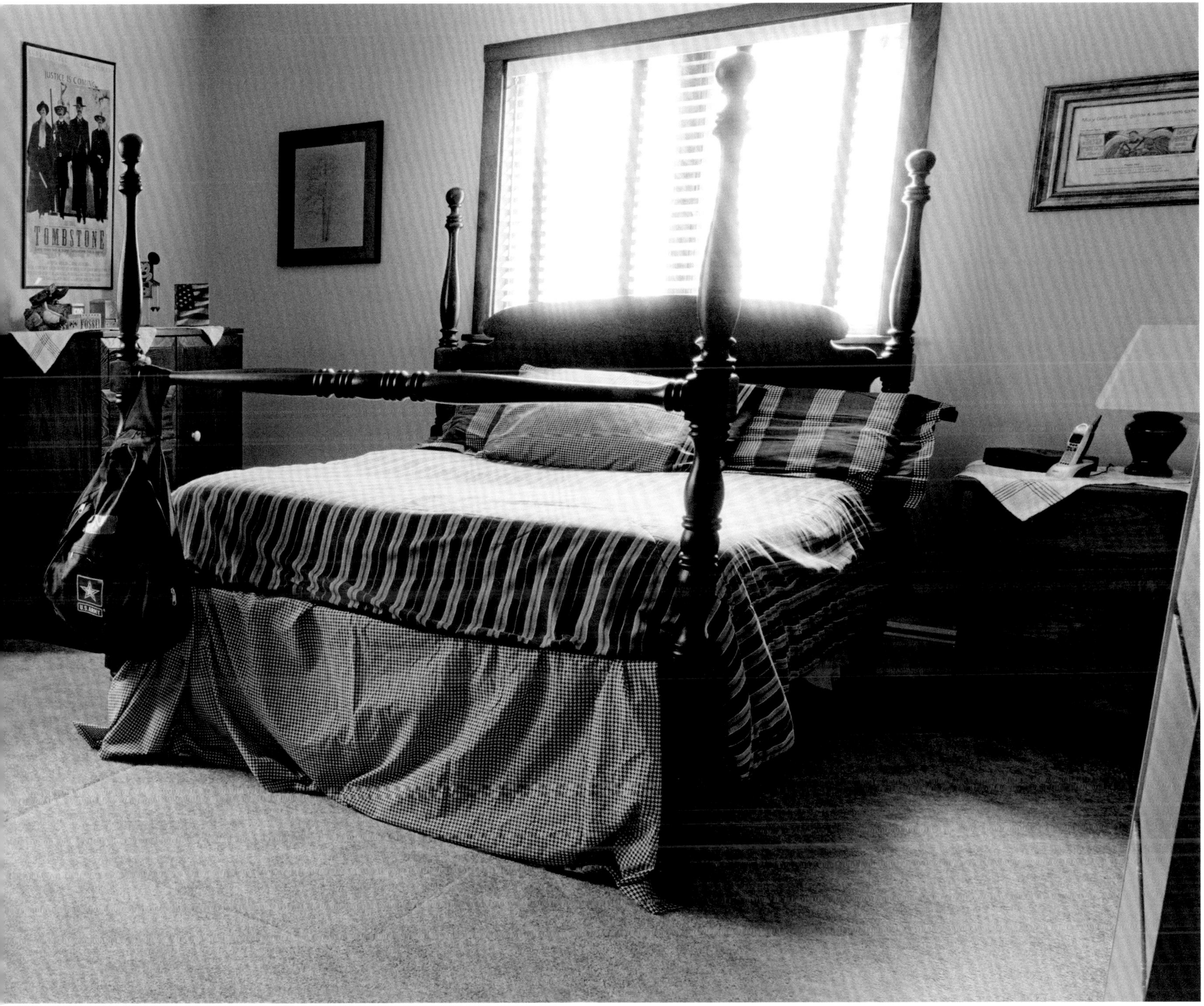

Army Special Forces Staff Sergeant Travis K. Hunsberger, 24, was killed by a roadside bomb on June 27, 2008, near Tarin Kowt, Afghanistan. He was from Goshen, Indiana. His bedroom was photographed in April 2011.

Marine Private First Class Josue Ibarra, 21, was killed by a roadside bomb on June 19, 2011, in Helmand province, Afghanistan. He was from Midland, Texas. His bedroom was photographed in December 2012.

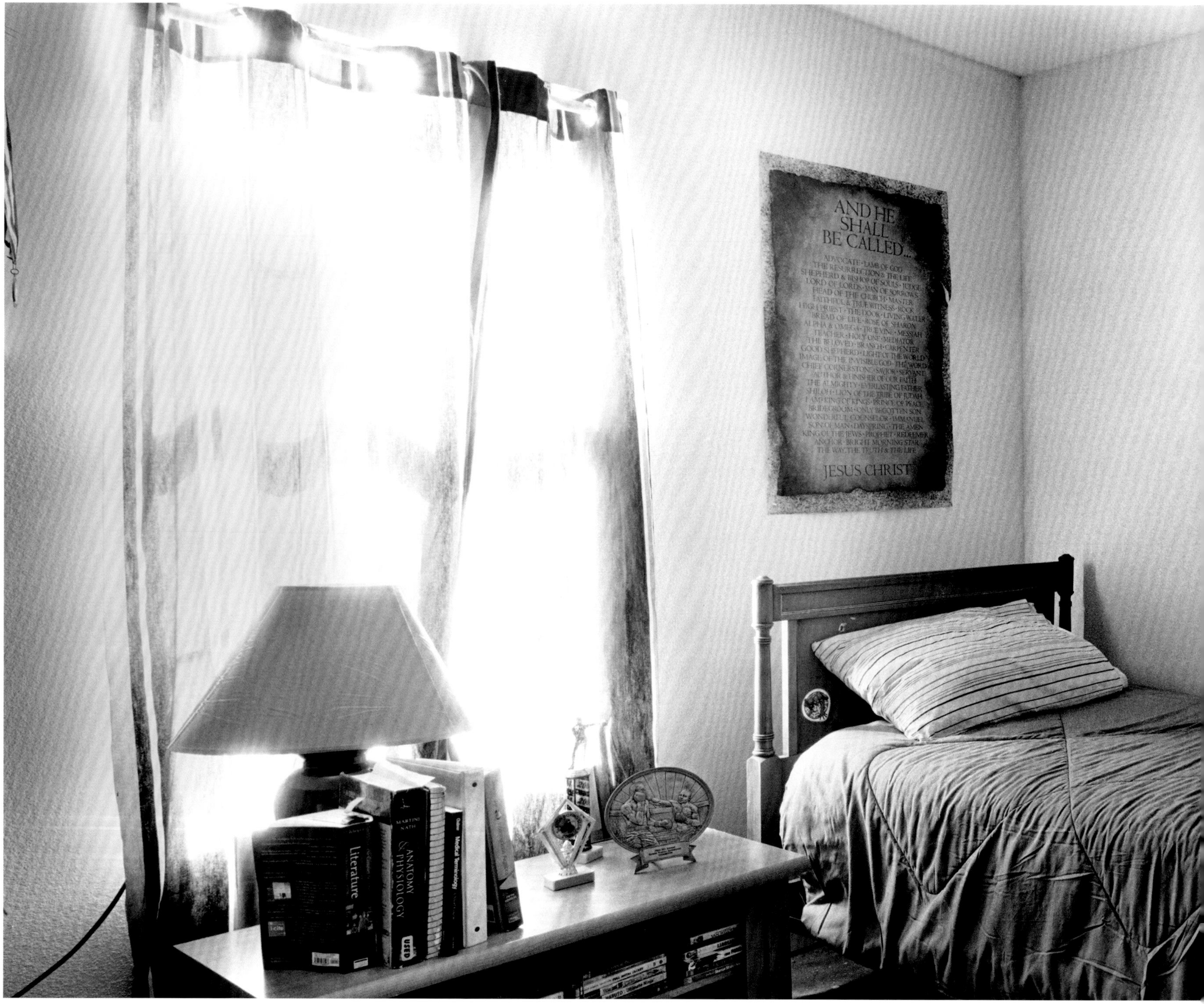

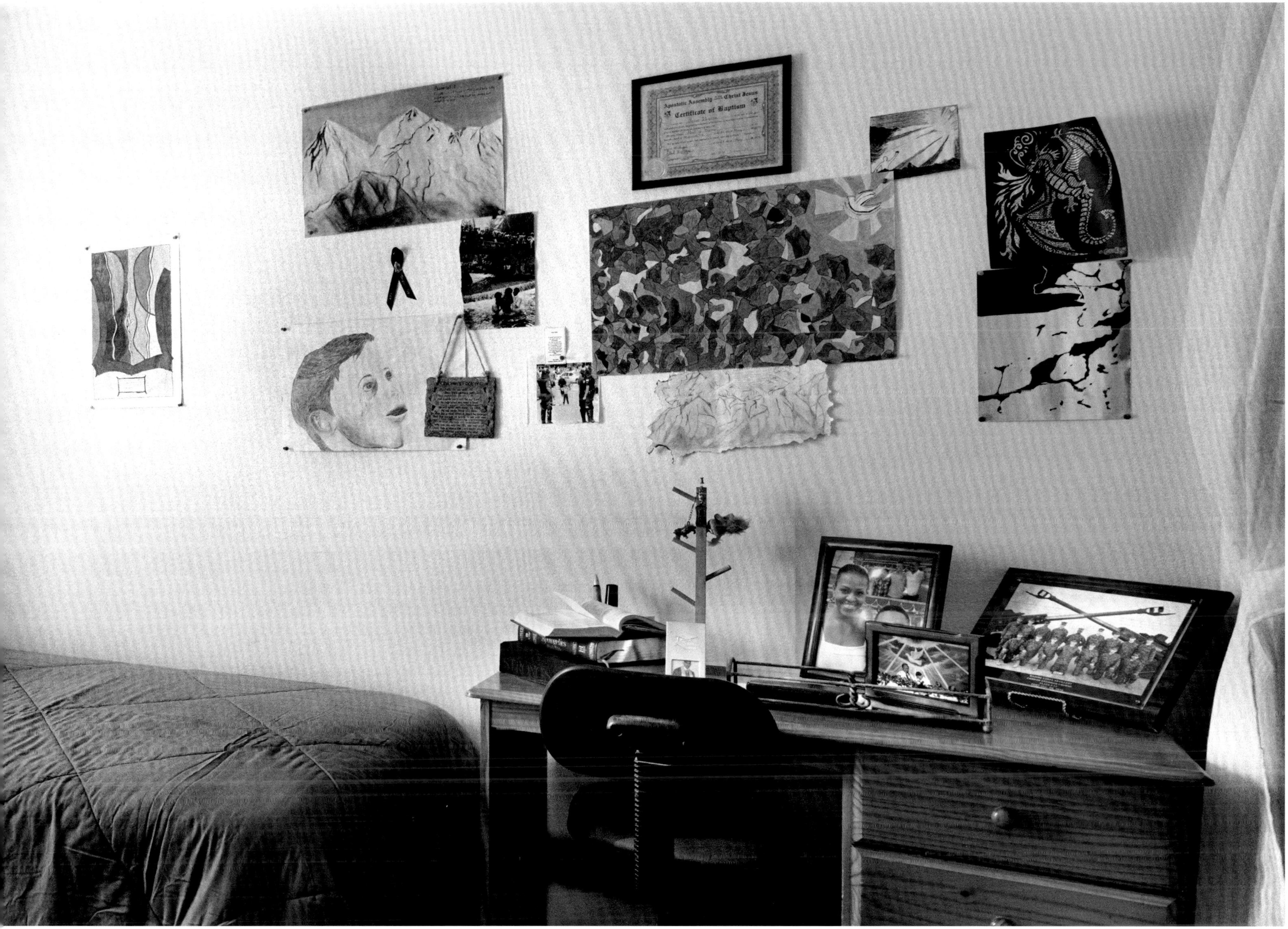
Certificate of Baptism

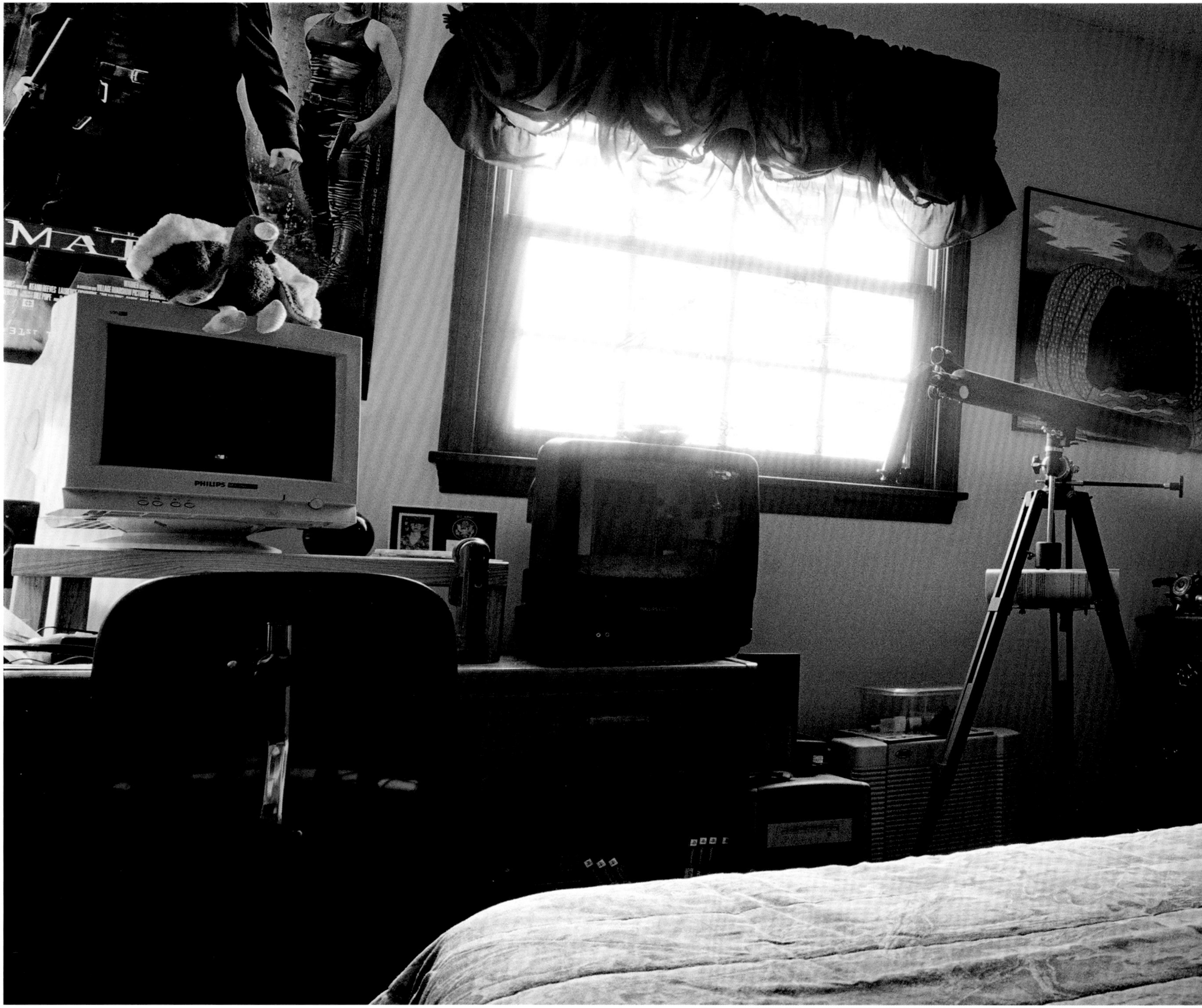

Army Private First Class Richard P. Langenbrunner, 19, killed himself on April 17, 2007, in Rustimayah, Iraq. He was from Fort Wayne, Indiana. His bedroom was photographed in February 2009.

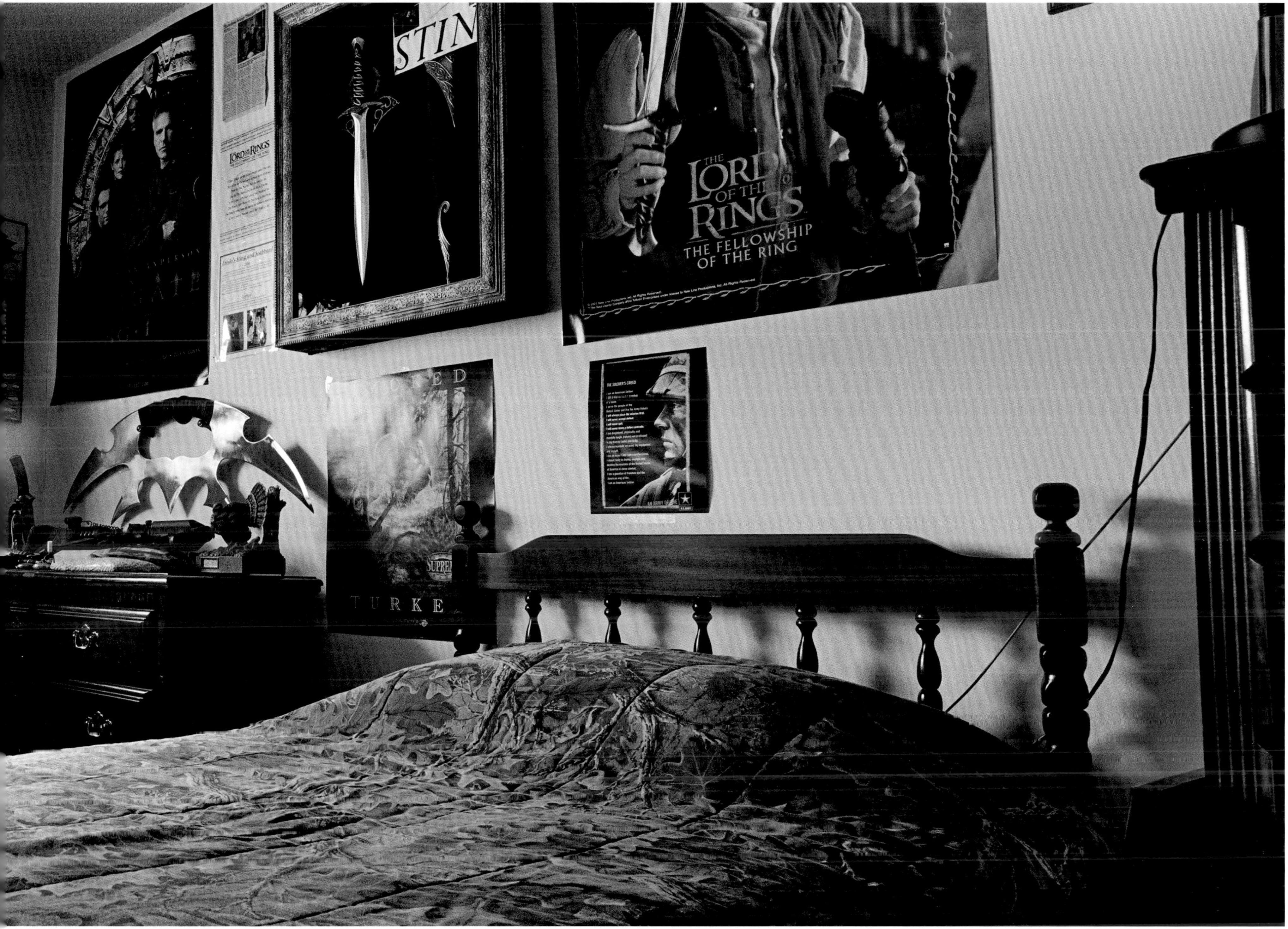
STIN
THE LORD OF THE RINGS
THE FELLOWSHIP OF THE RING
TURKE

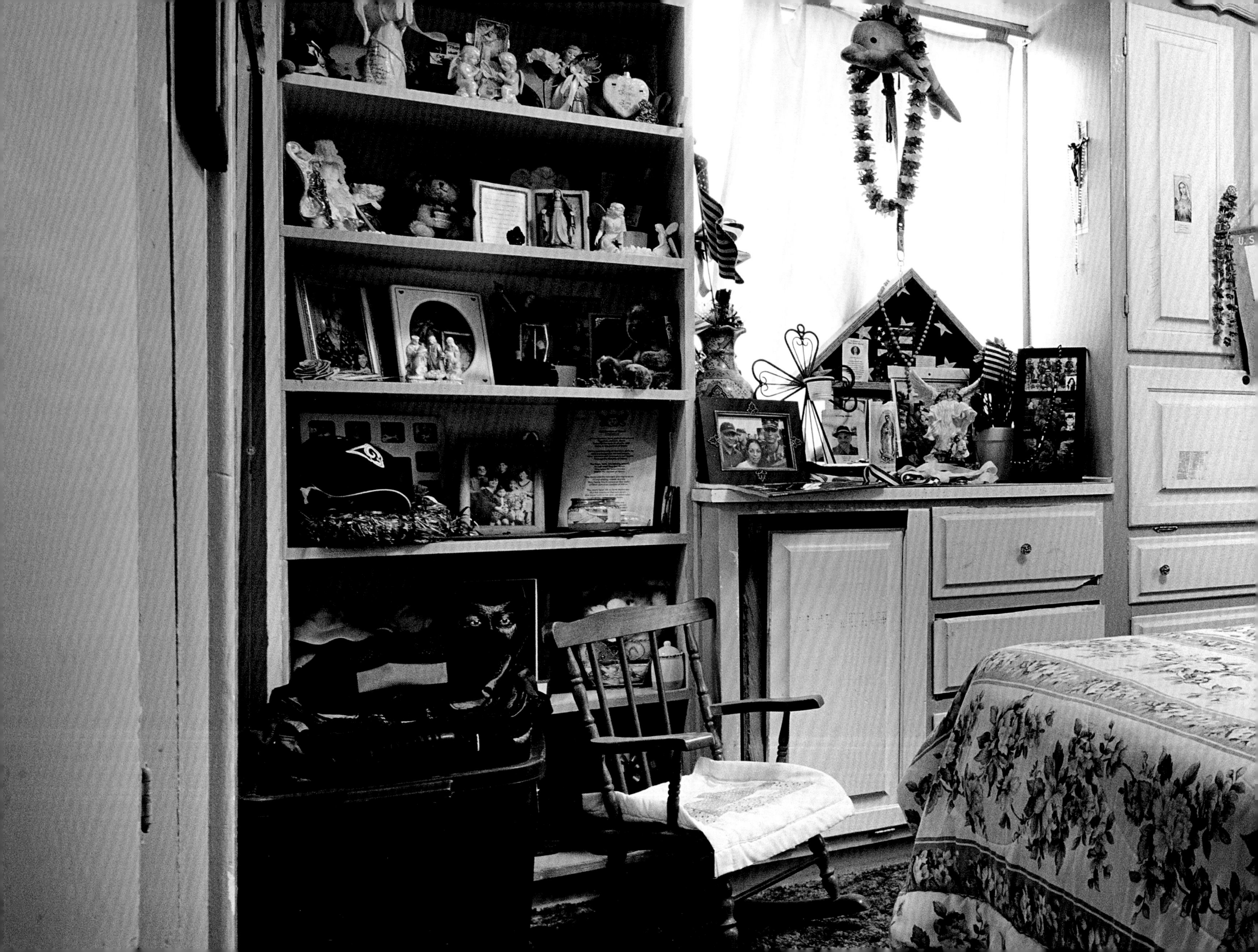

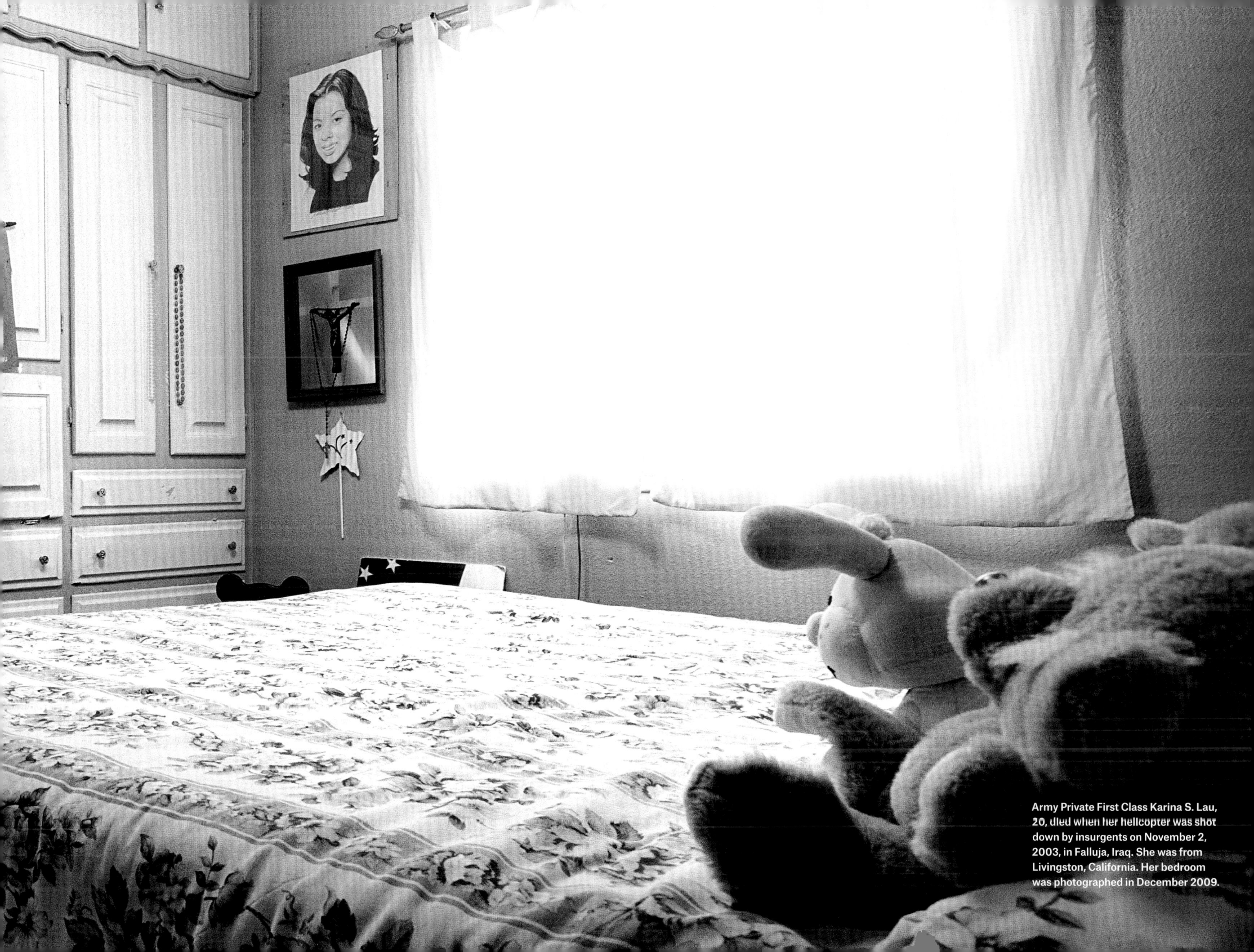

Army Private First Class Karina S. Lau, 20, died when her helicopter was shot down by insurgents on November 2, 2003, in Falluja, Iraq. She was from Livingston, California. Her bedroom was photographed in December 2009.

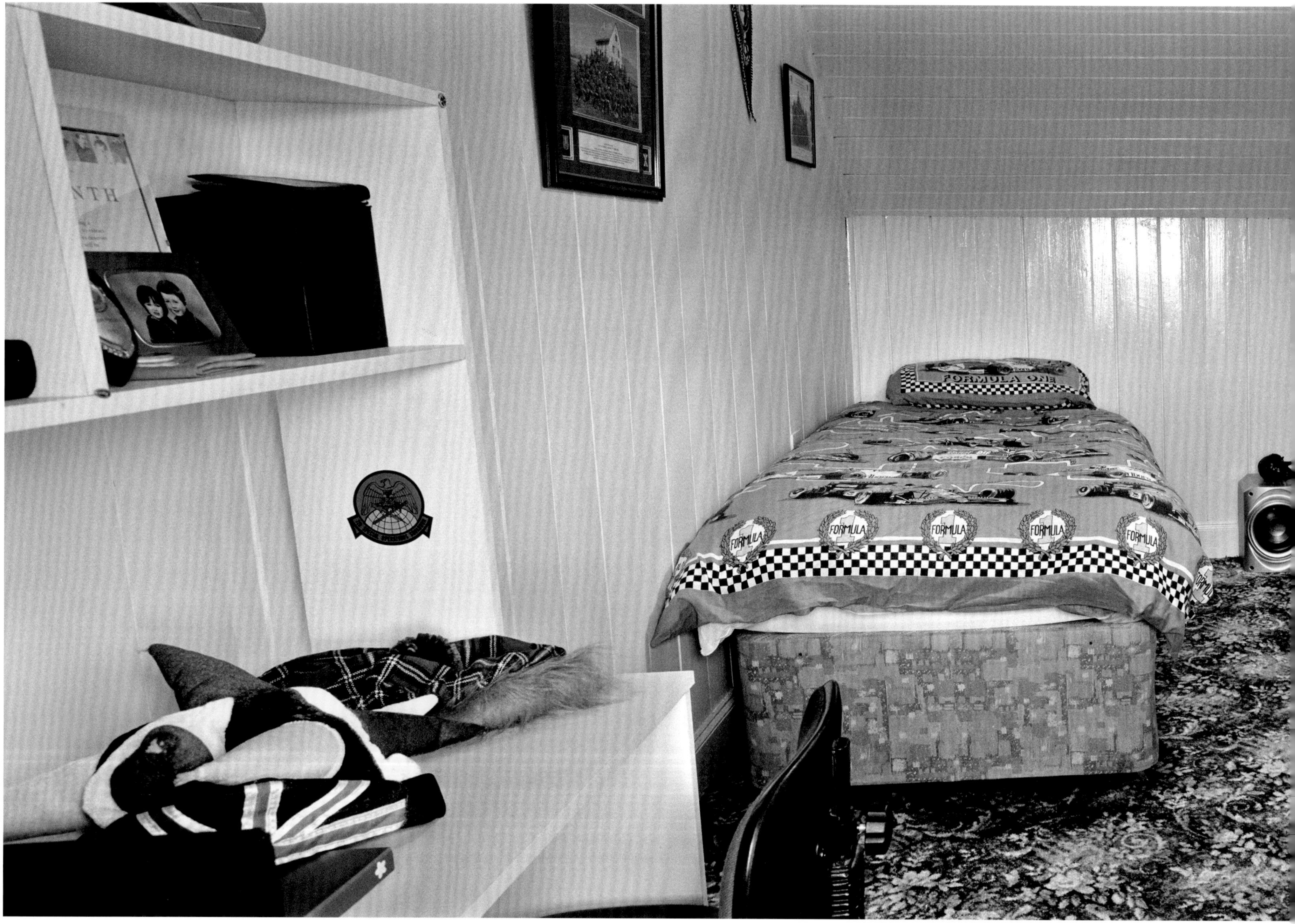
FORMULA ONE
FORMULA

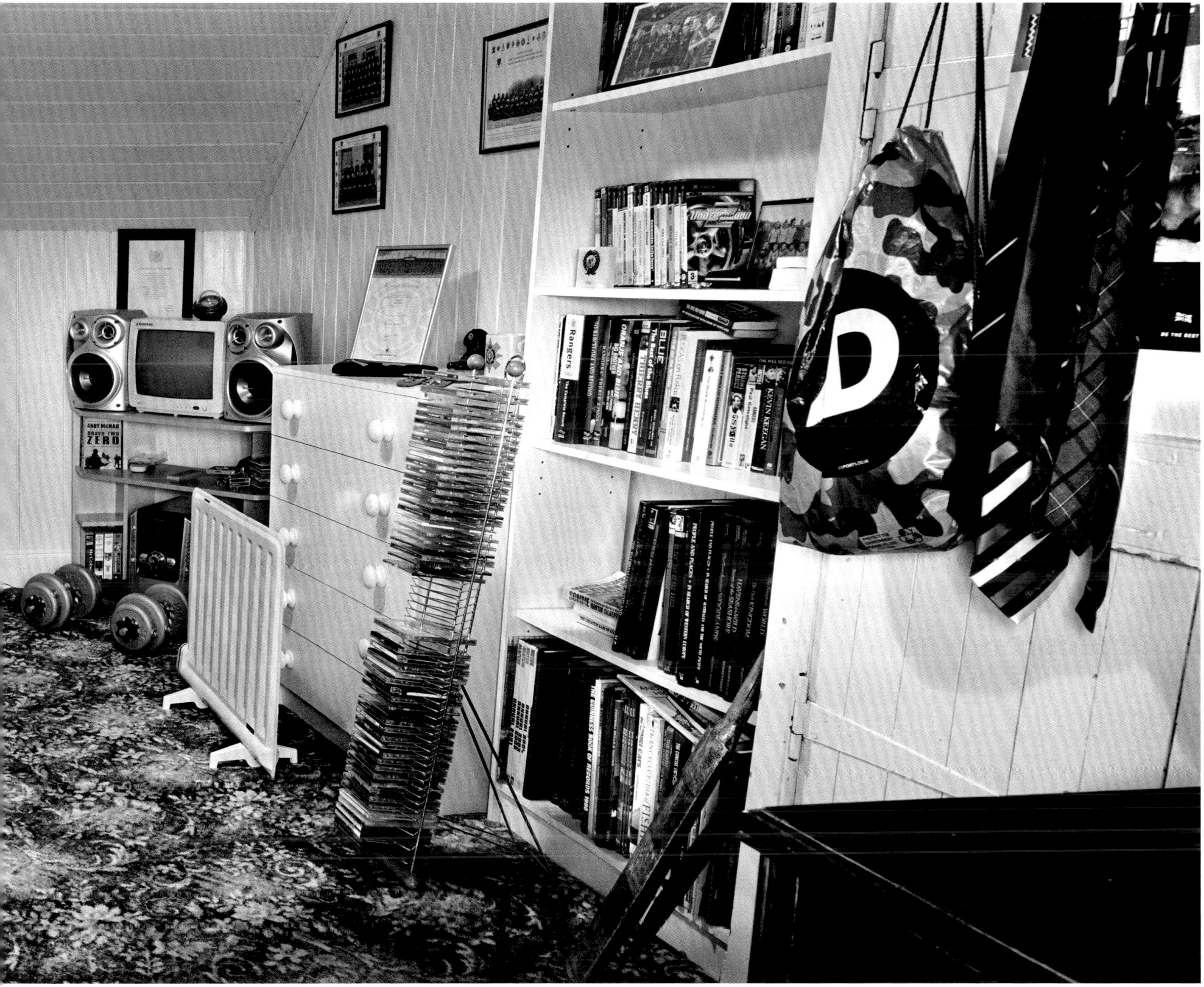

Private Robert McLaren, 20, was killed by a roadside bomb on June 11, 2009, in Helmand, Afghanistan. He was from Kintra Fionnphort, Isle of Mull, Scotland. His bedroom was photographed in March 2011.

Stabsgefreiter Konstantin A. Menz, 22, was killed by a rogue Afghan soldier on February 18, 2011, in Baghlan, Afghanistan. He was from Backnang, Germany. His bedroom was photographed in February 2012.

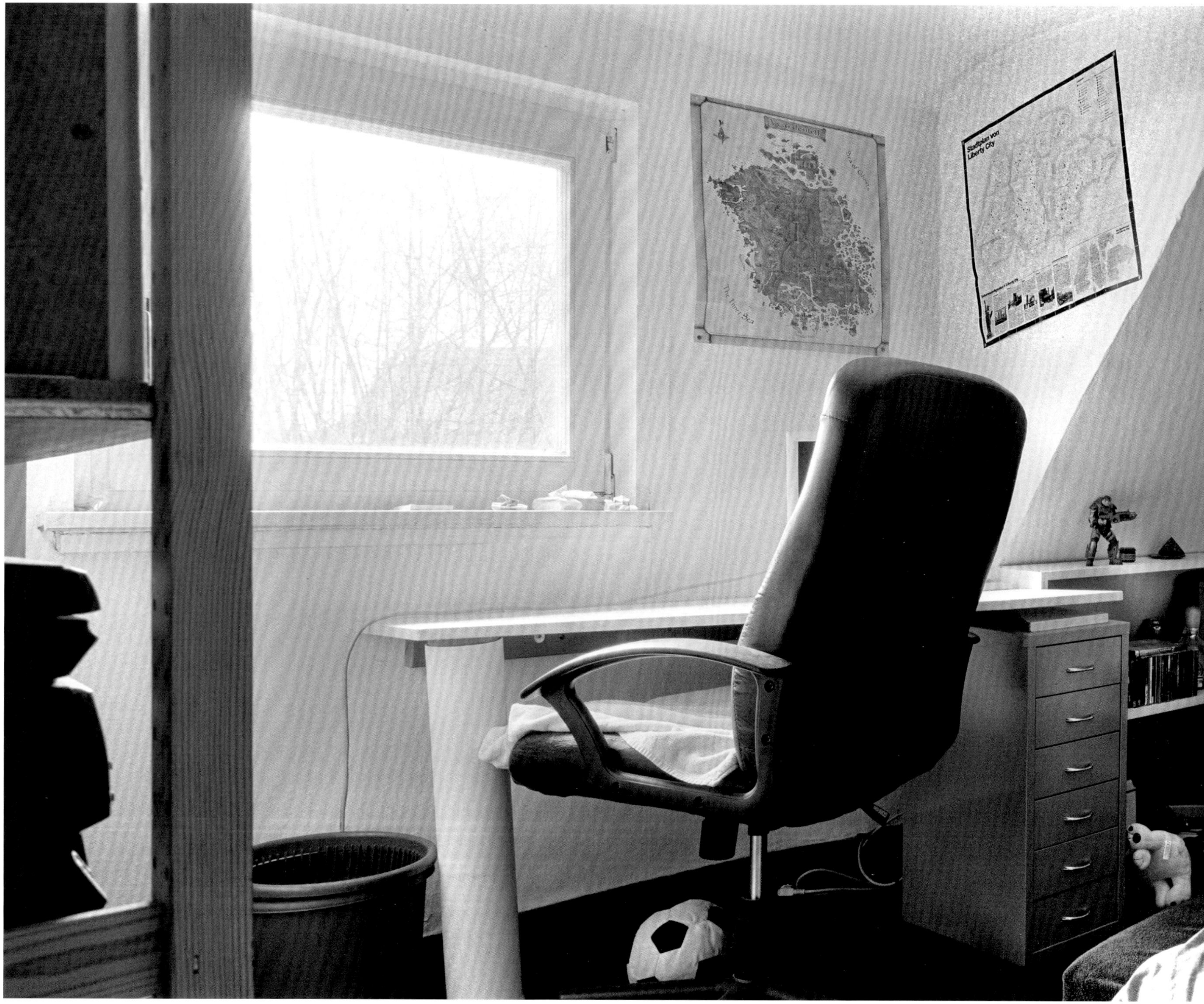

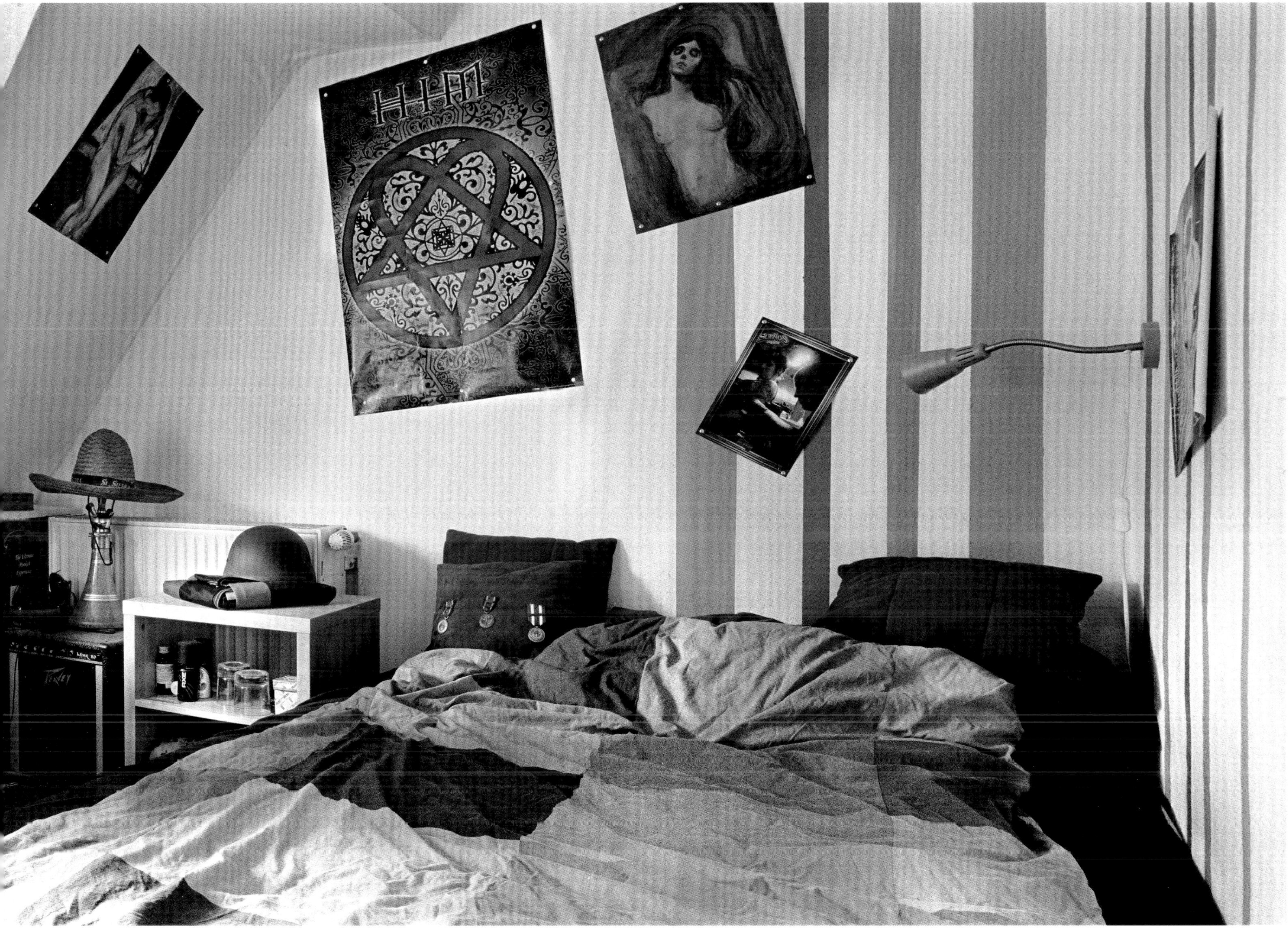
HIM

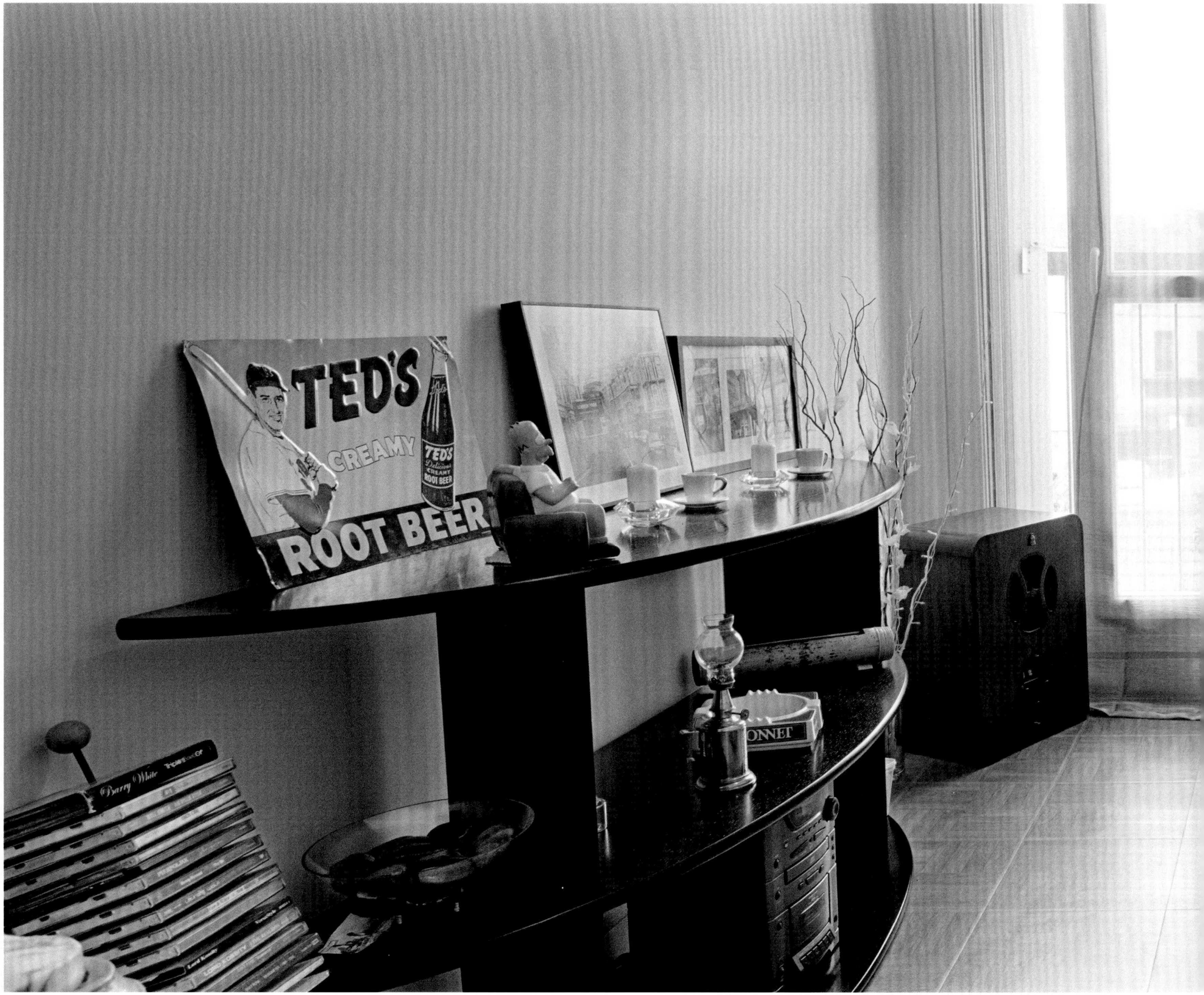

Marine Corporal Chef Jean-Nicolas Panezyck, 25, was killed by small arms fire on August 23, 2010, in Tagab, Afghanistan. He was from Versailles, France. His bedroom was photographed in March 2011.

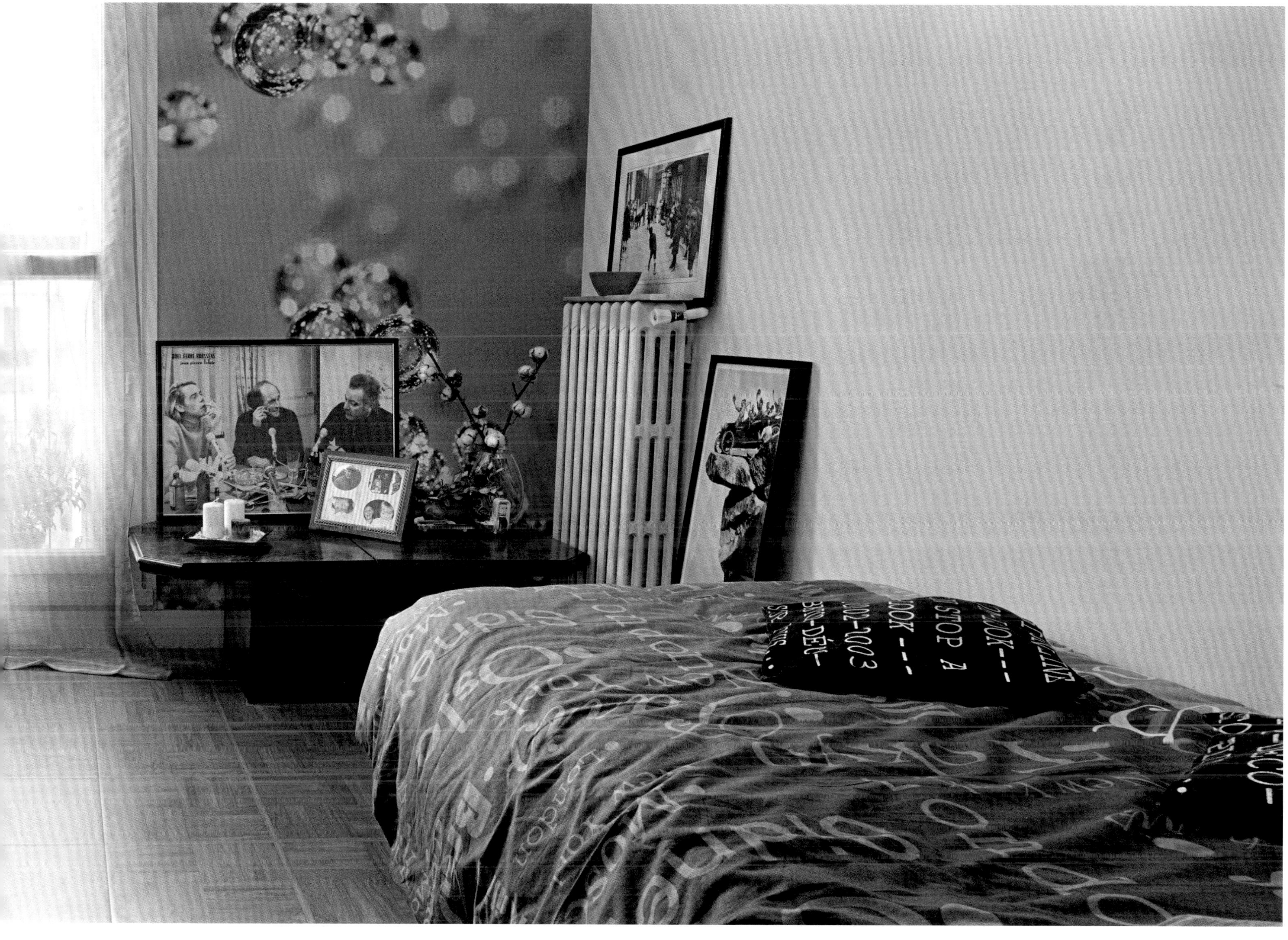

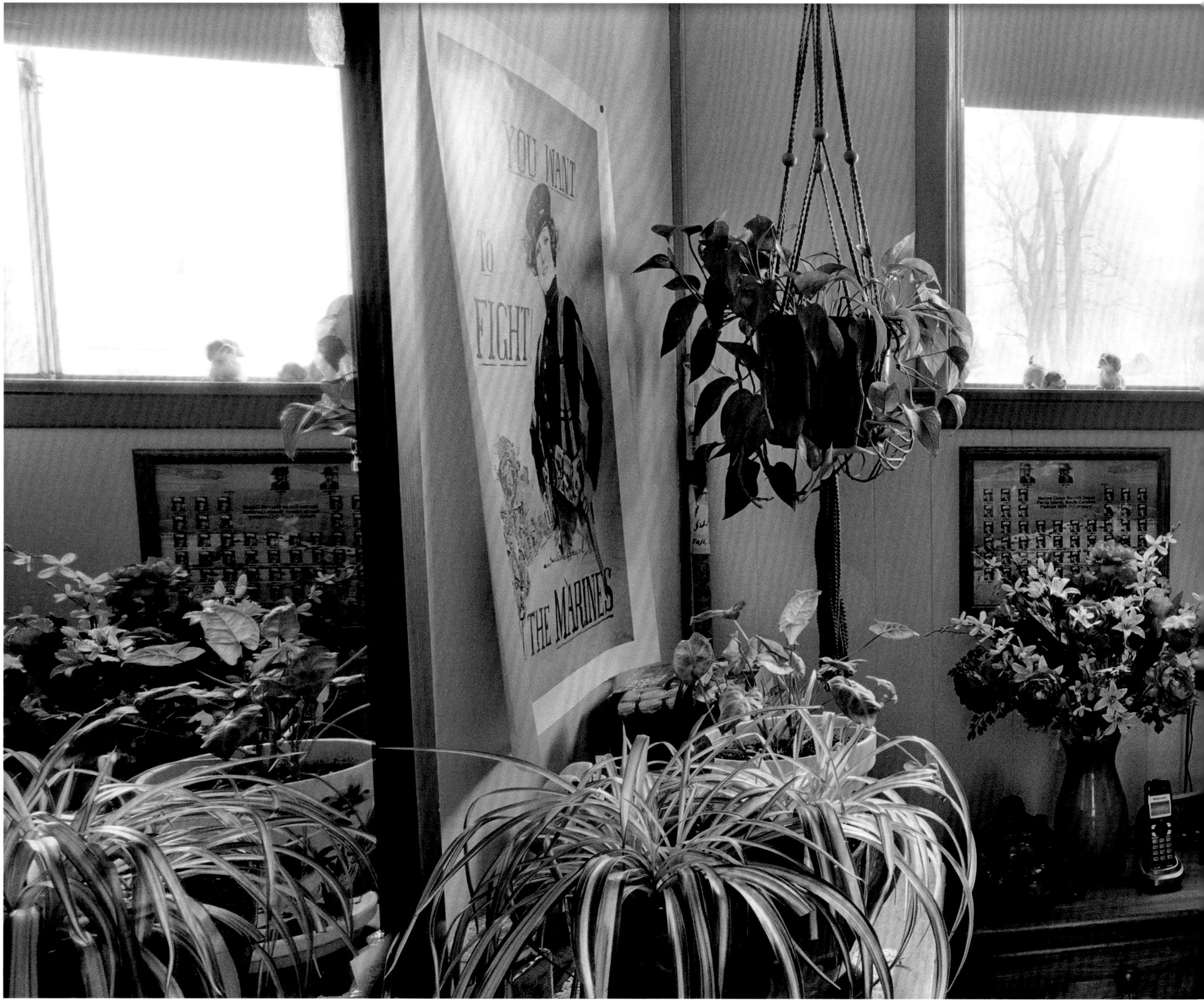

Marine Corporal Jennifer M. Parcell, 20, was killed by a suicide bomber on February 7, 2007, in Anbar province, Iraq. She was from Bel Air, Maryland. Her bedroom was photographed in March 2010.

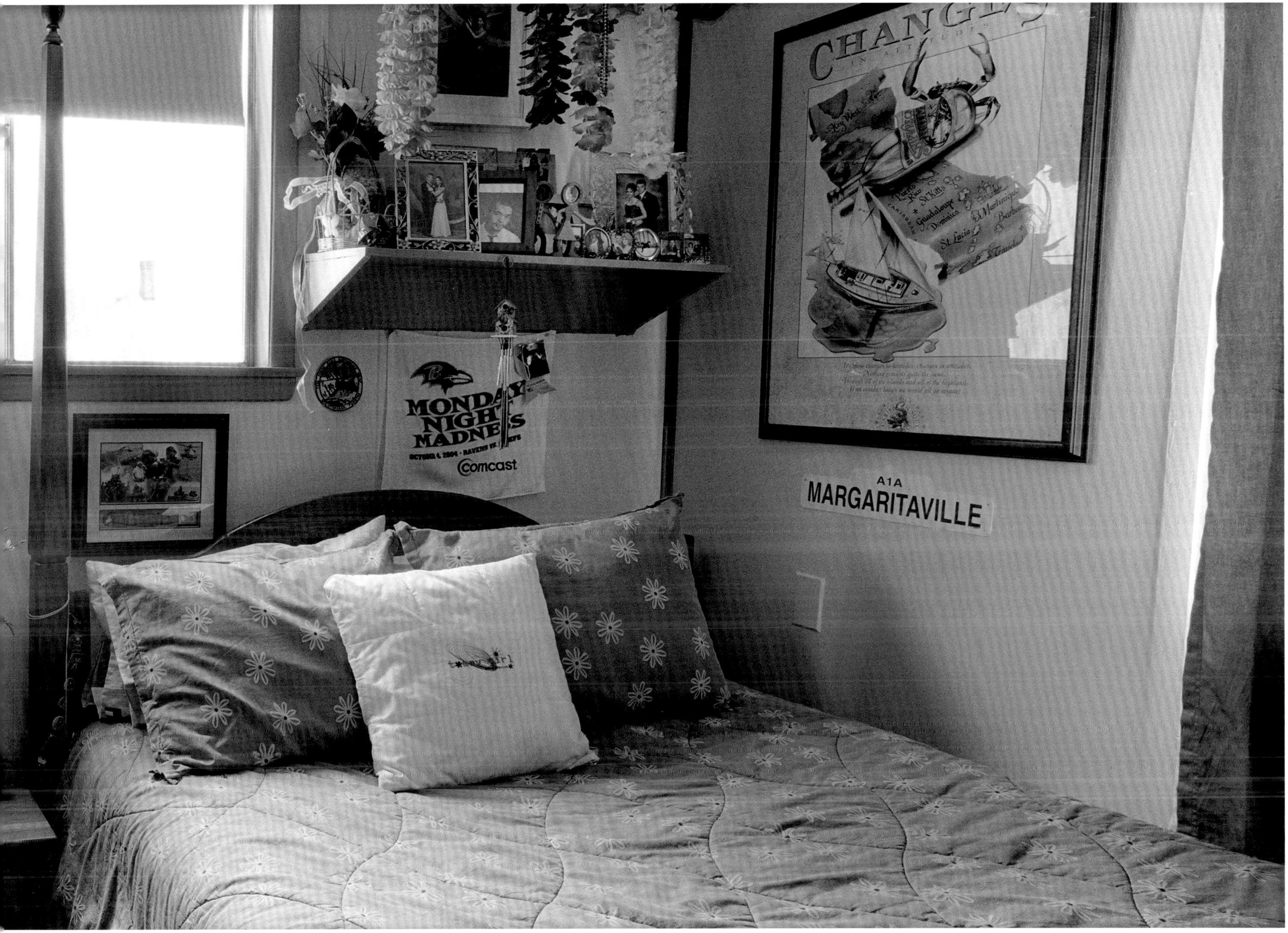
CHANGES
Comcast
A1A
MARGARITAVILLE

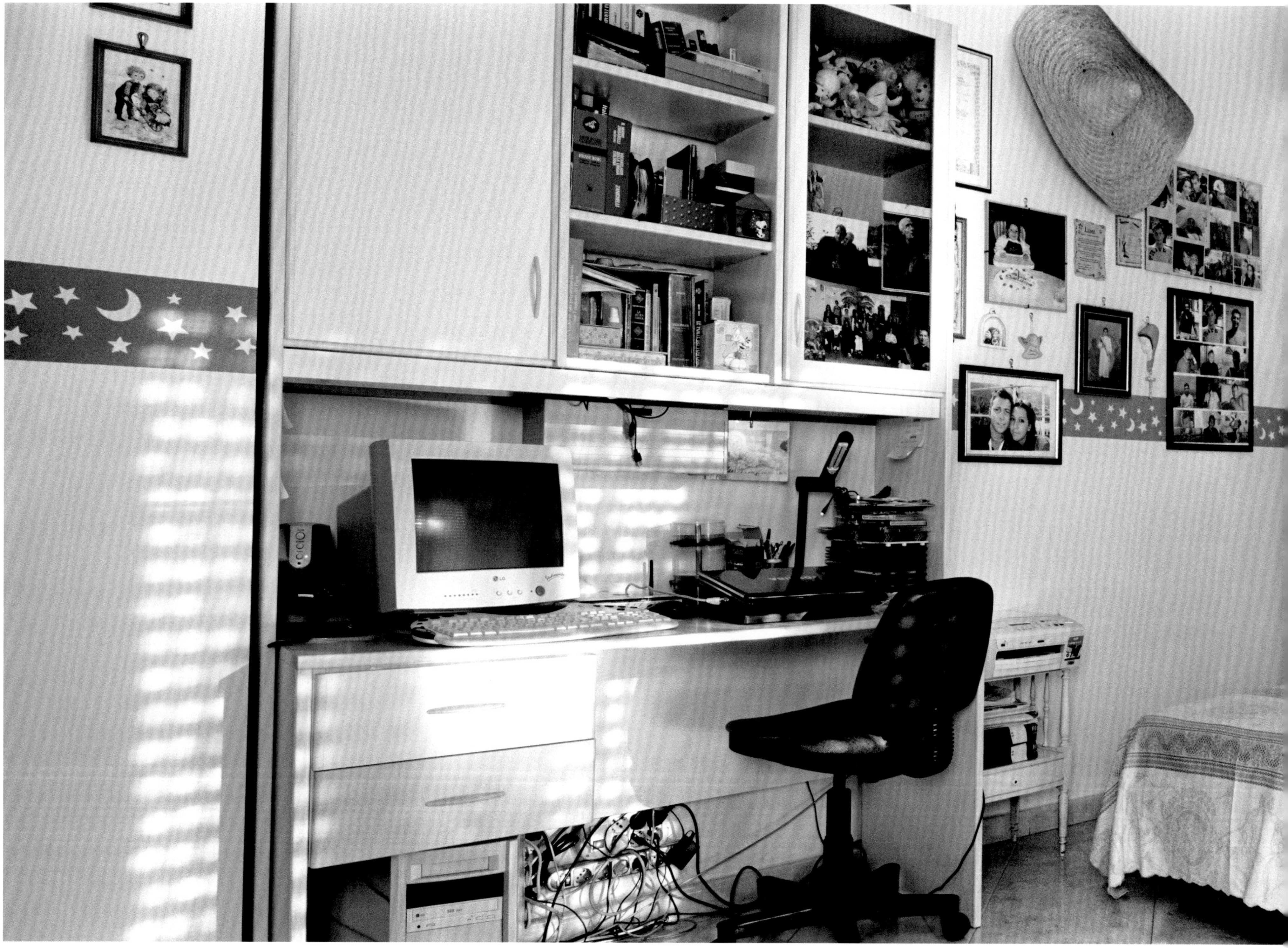

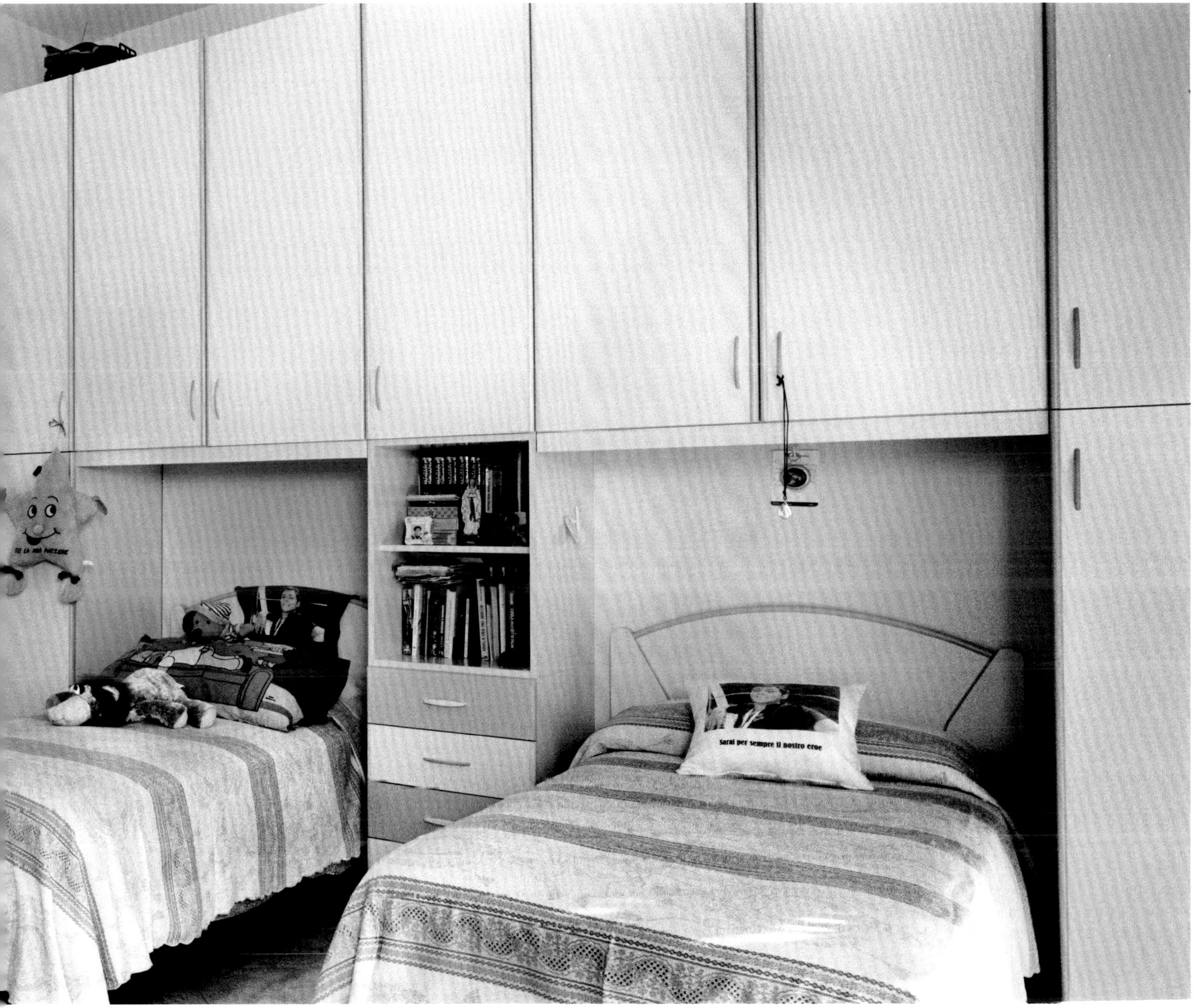

Caporal Luigi Pascazio, 24, was killed by a roadside bomb on May 17, 2010, near Herat, Afghanistan. He was from Bitetto, Bari, Italy. His bedroom was photographed in August 2011.

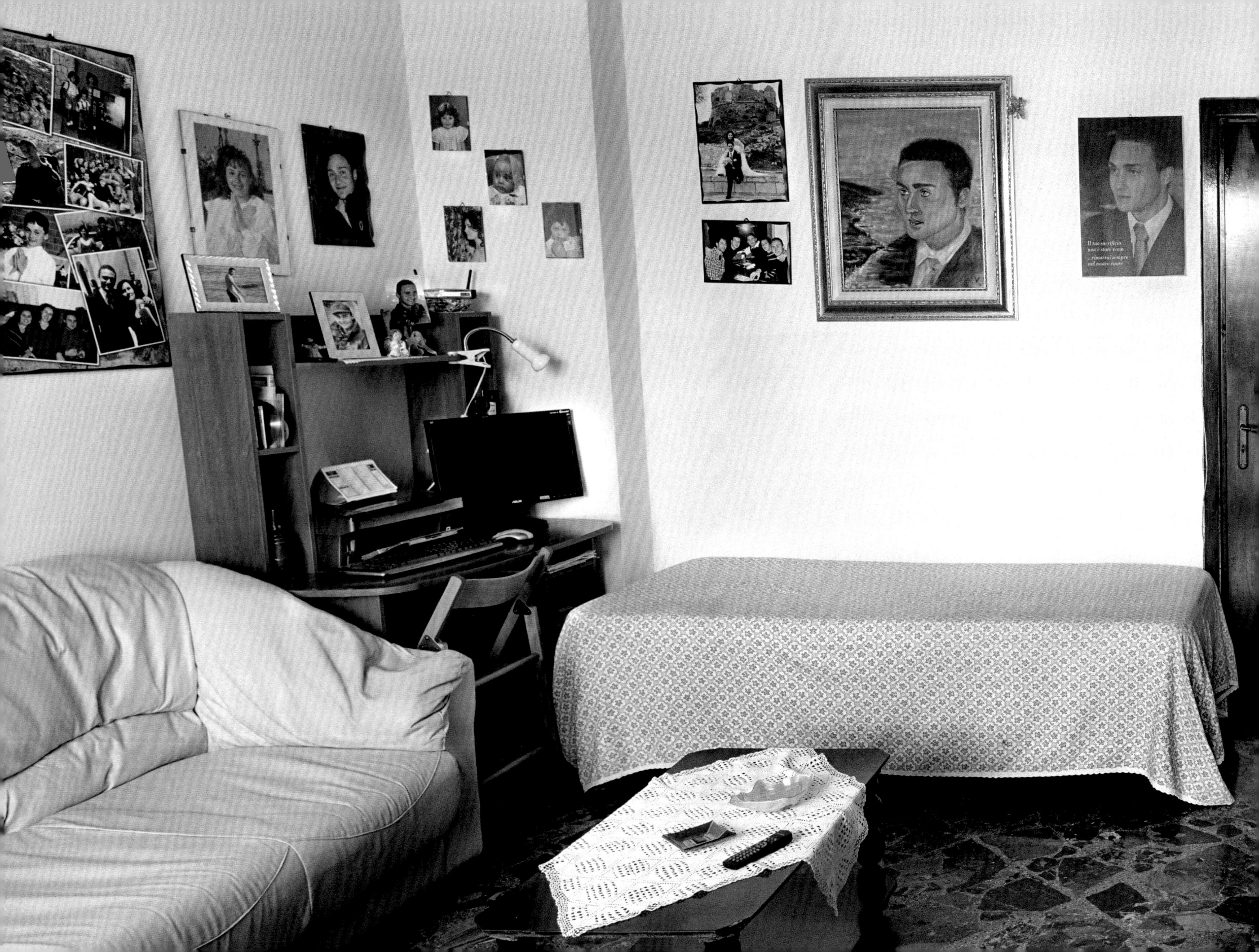
Il tuo sacrificio
non è stato vano
...rimarrai sempre
nel nostro cuore

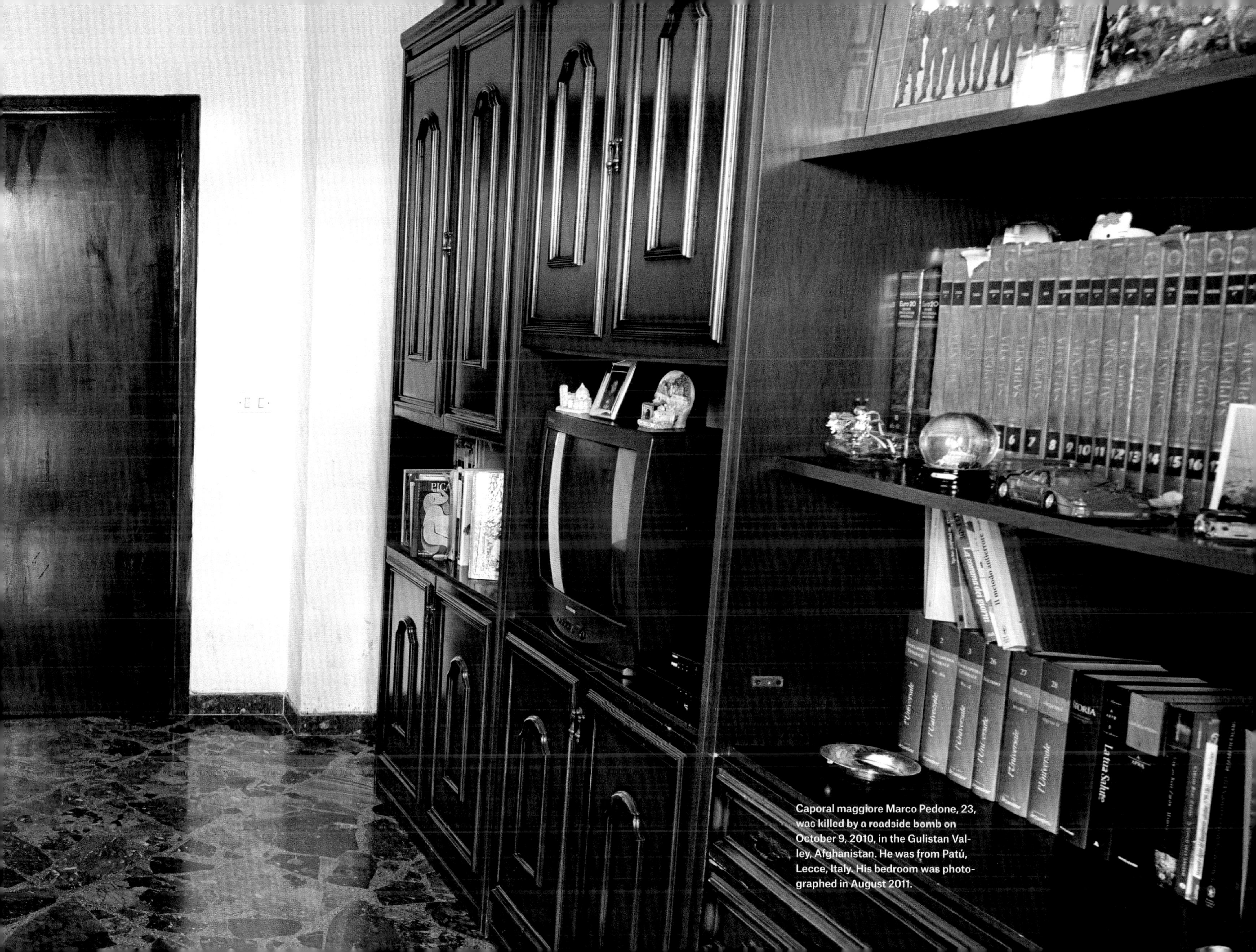

Caporal maggiore Marco Pedone, 23, was killed by a roadside bomb on October 9, 2010, in the Gulistan Valley, Afghanistan. He was from Patú, Lecce, Italy. His bedroom was photographed in August 2011.

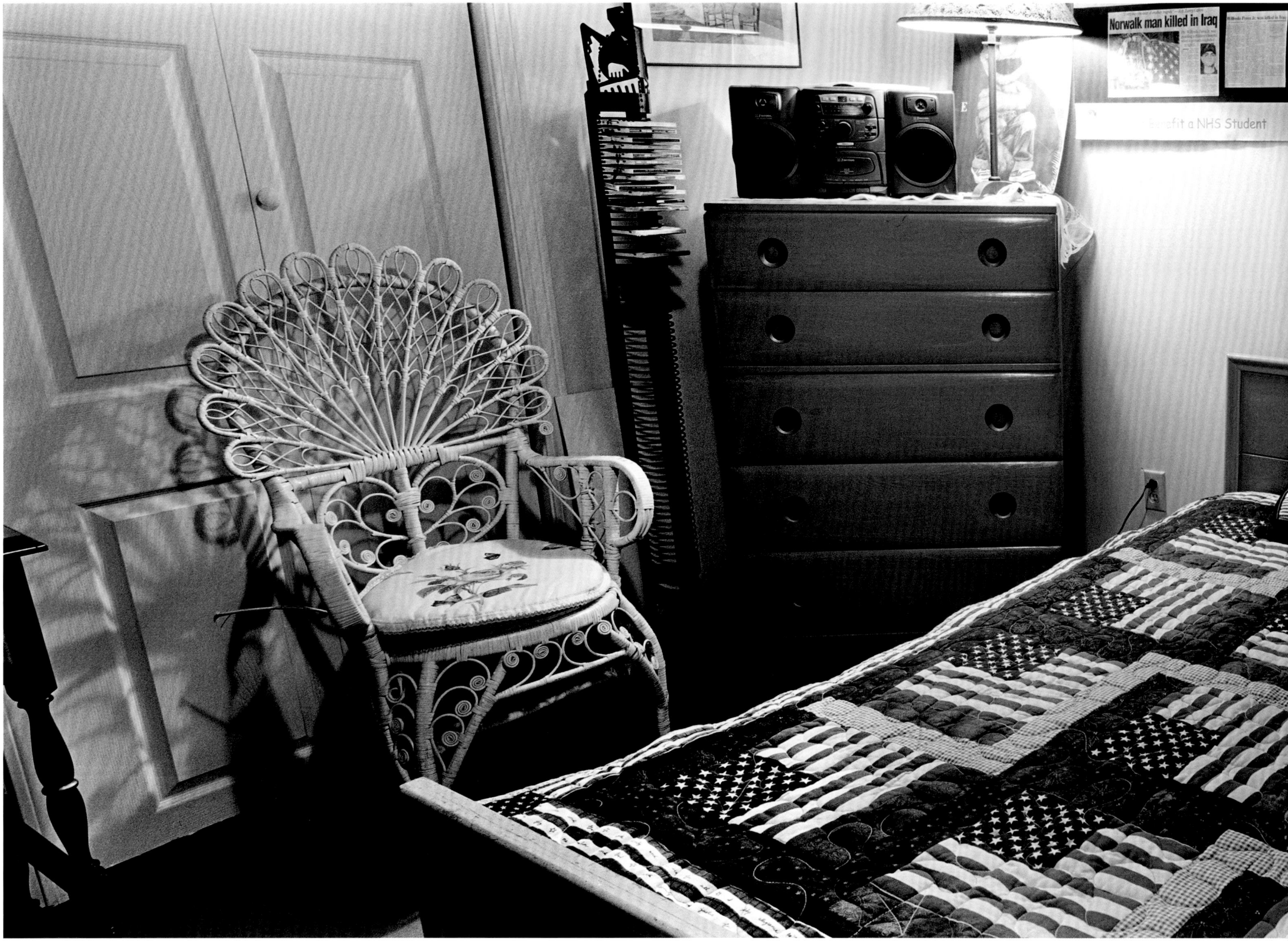
Norwalk man killed in Iraq
Benefit a NHS Student

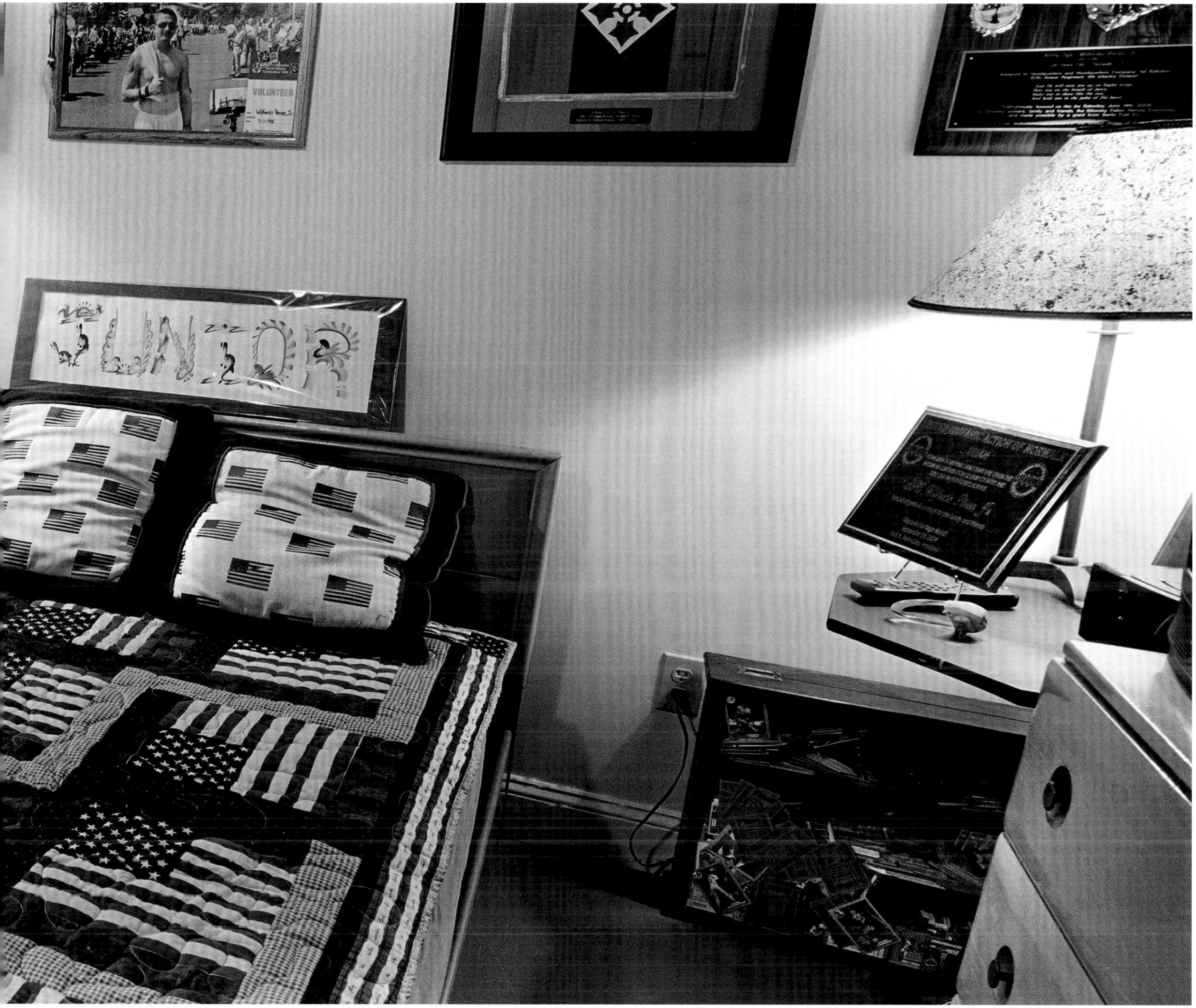

Army Specialist Wilfredo Perez Jr., 24, was killed in a grenade attack on July 26, 2003, in Baquba, Iraq. He was from Norwalk, Connecticut. His bedroom was photographed in January 2010.

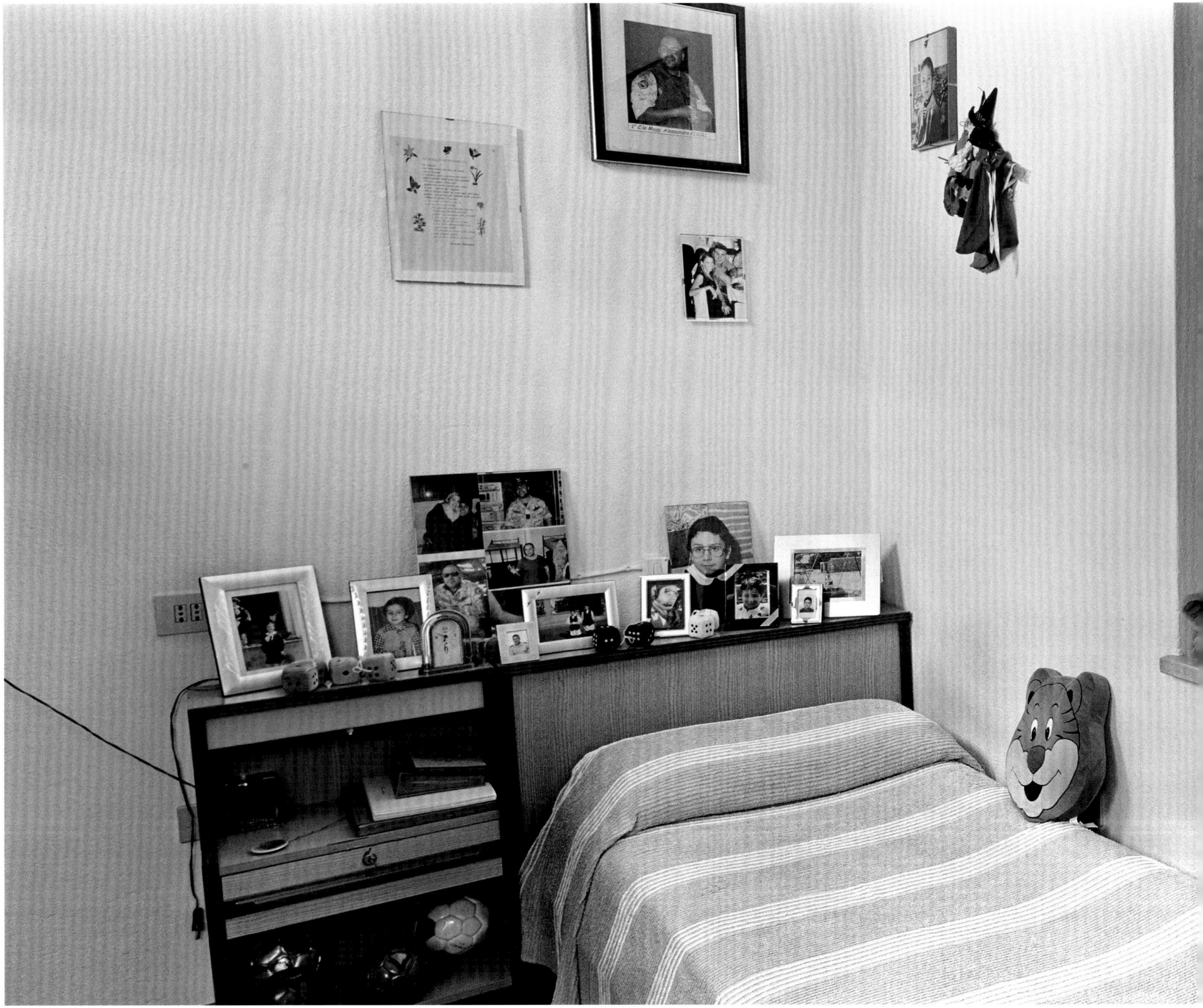

Primo caporal maggiore Alessandro Pibiri, 24, was killed by a roadside bomb on June 5, 2006, in Naseriya, Iraq. He was from Selargius, Sardegna, Italy. His bedroom was photographed in August 2011.

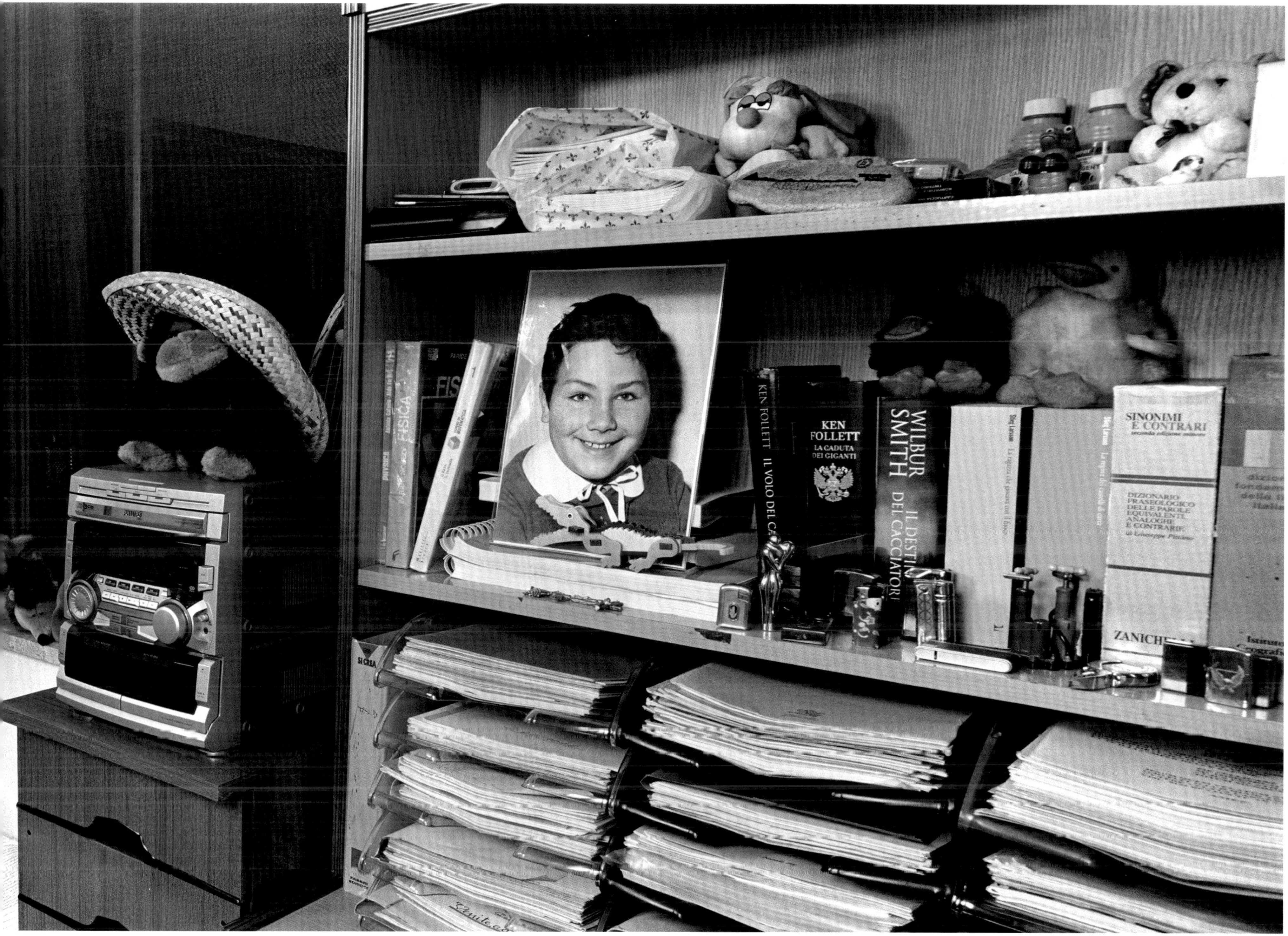
KEN FOLLETT
IL VOLO DEL CA
KEN FOLLETT
LA CADUTA DEI GIGANTI
WILBUR SMITH
SINONIMI E CONTRARI
seconda edizione minore
DIZIONARIO FRASEOLOGICO DELLE PAROLE EQUIVALENTI, ANALOGHE E CONTRARIE
FISICA

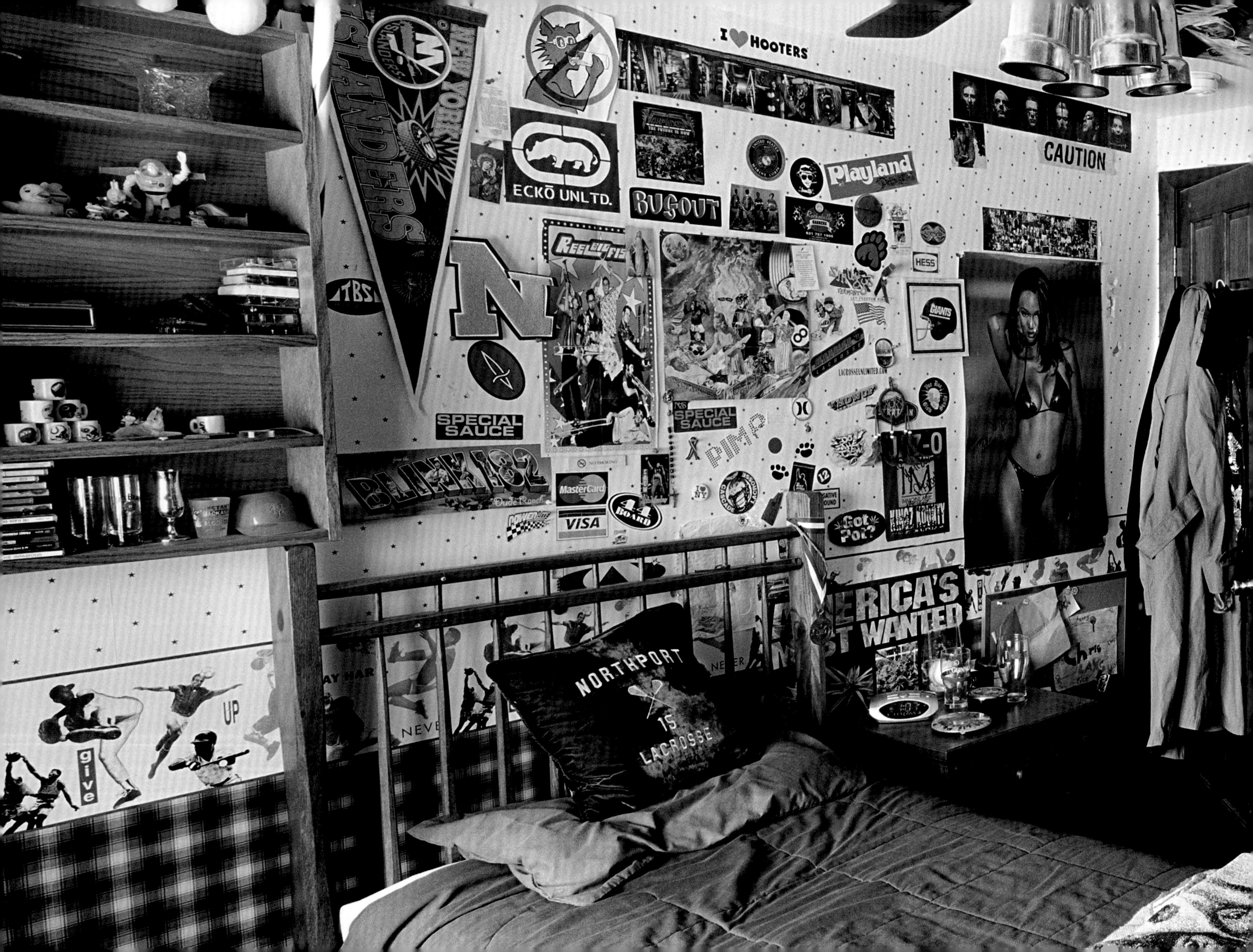
NEW YORK
ISLANDERS
I ♥ HOOTERS
ECKŌ UNLTD.
BUGOUT
Playland
CAUTION
TBS
HESS
GIANTS
SPECIAL SAUCE
SPECIAL SAUCE
BLINK 182
PIMP
MasterCard
VISA
44 BOARD
WANTED
NORTHPORT
15
LACROSSE
UP
give
NEVER

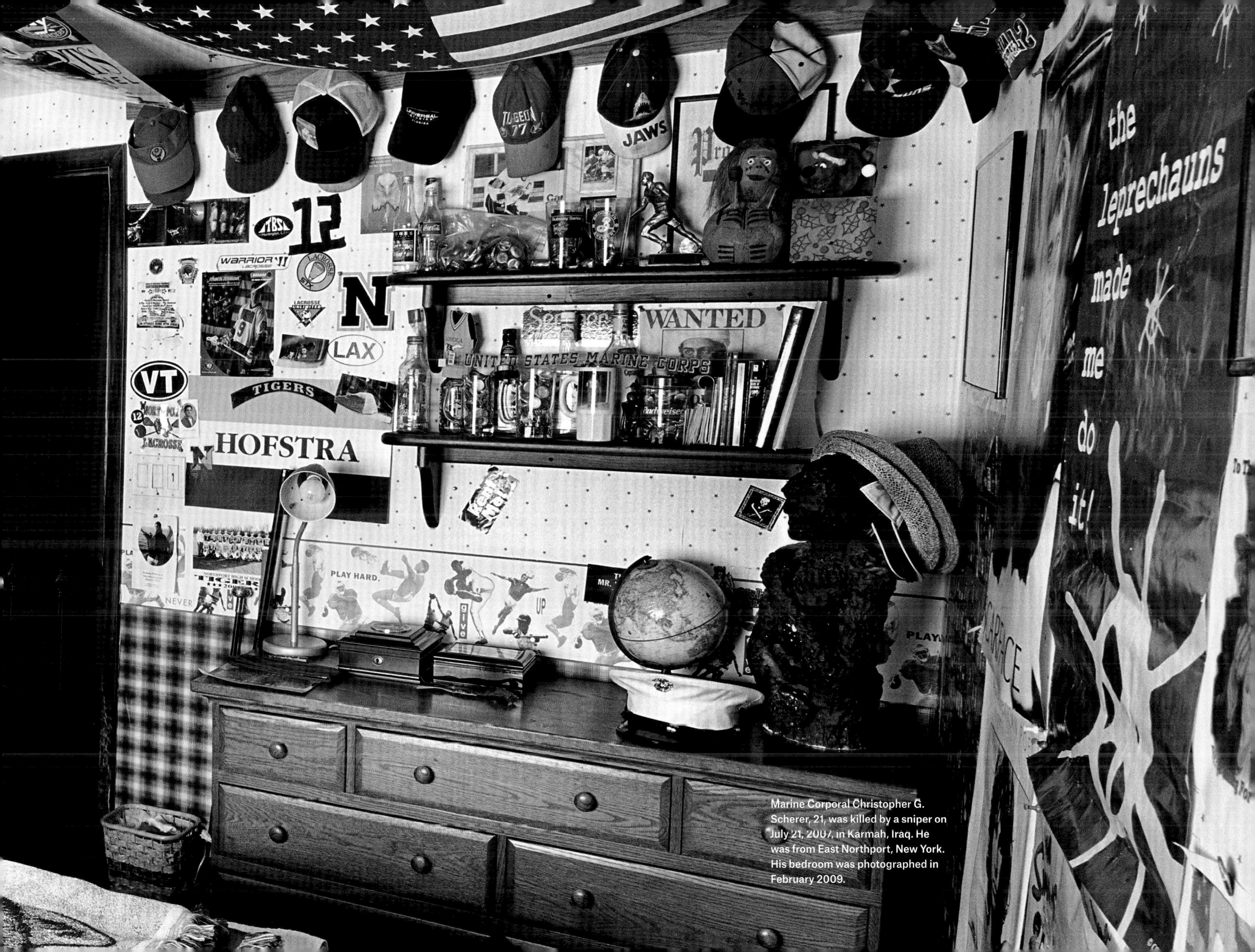

Marine Corporal Christopher G. Scherer, 21, was killed by a sniper on July 21, 2007, in Karmah, Iraq. He was from East Northport, New York. His bedroom was photographed in February 2009.

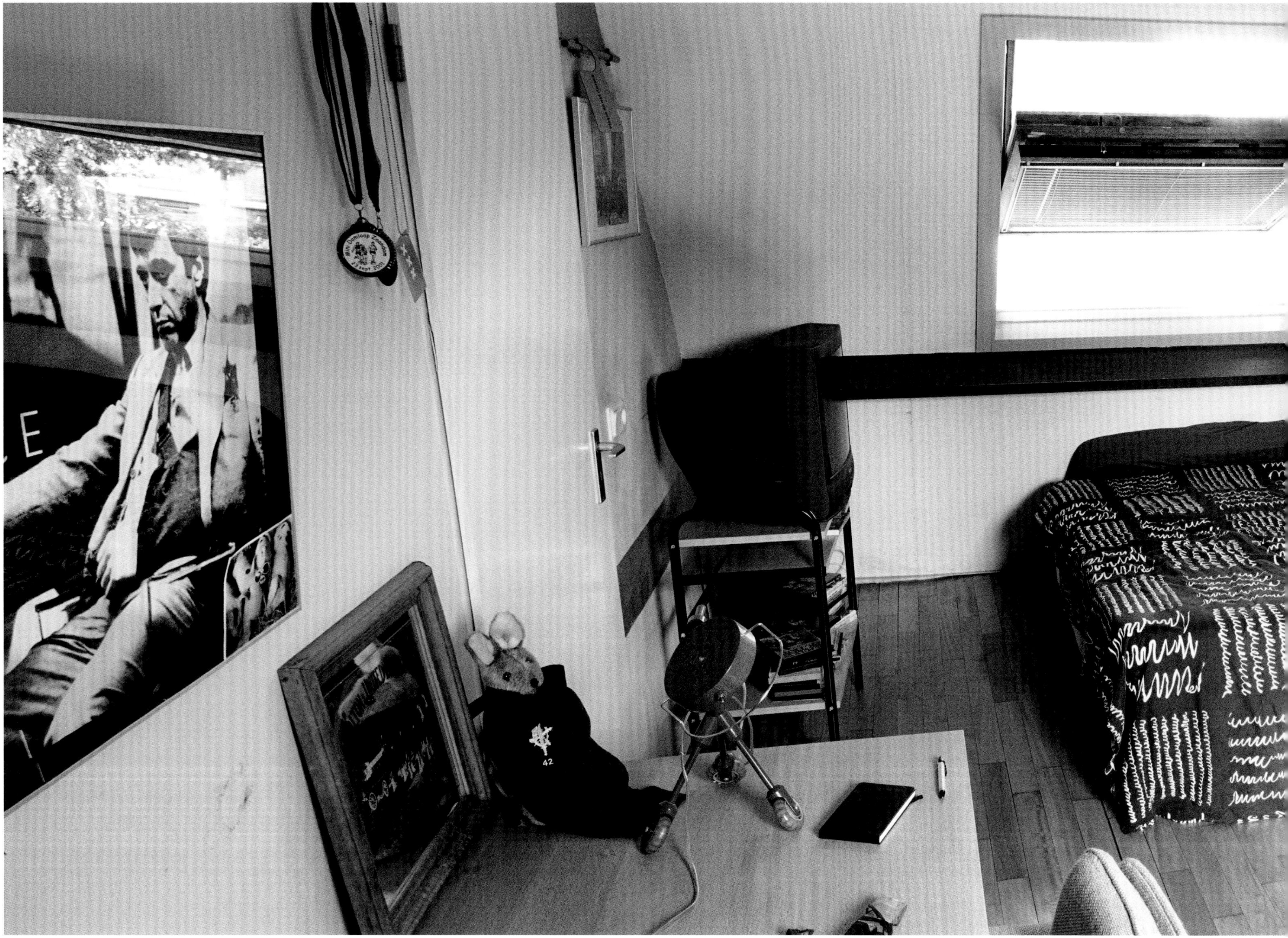

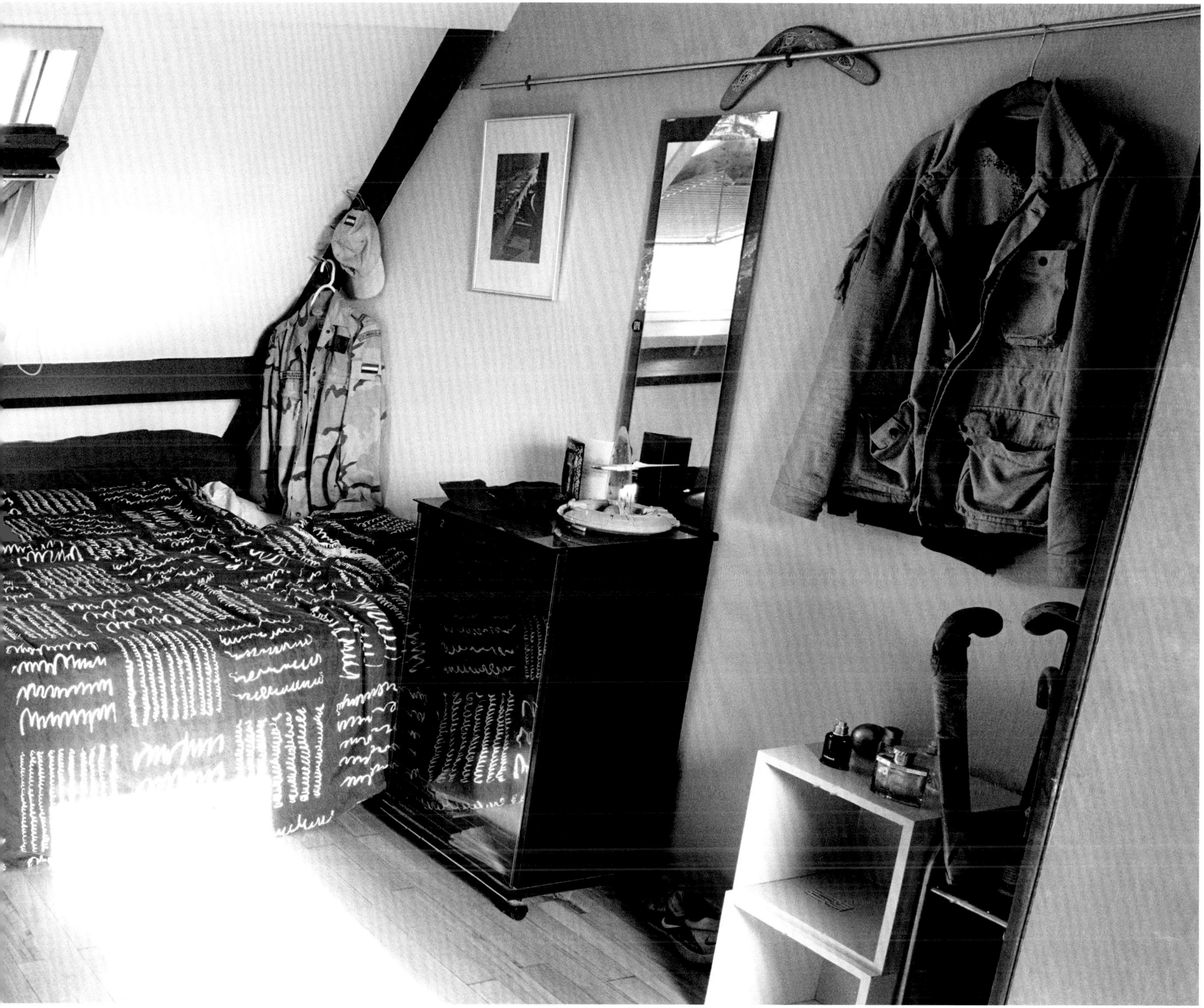

Soldier First Class Timo Smeehuijzen, 20, was killed by a suicide bomber on June 15, 2007, in Tarin Kowt, Afghanistan. He was from Amsterdam, The Netherlands. His bedroom was photographed in October 2010.

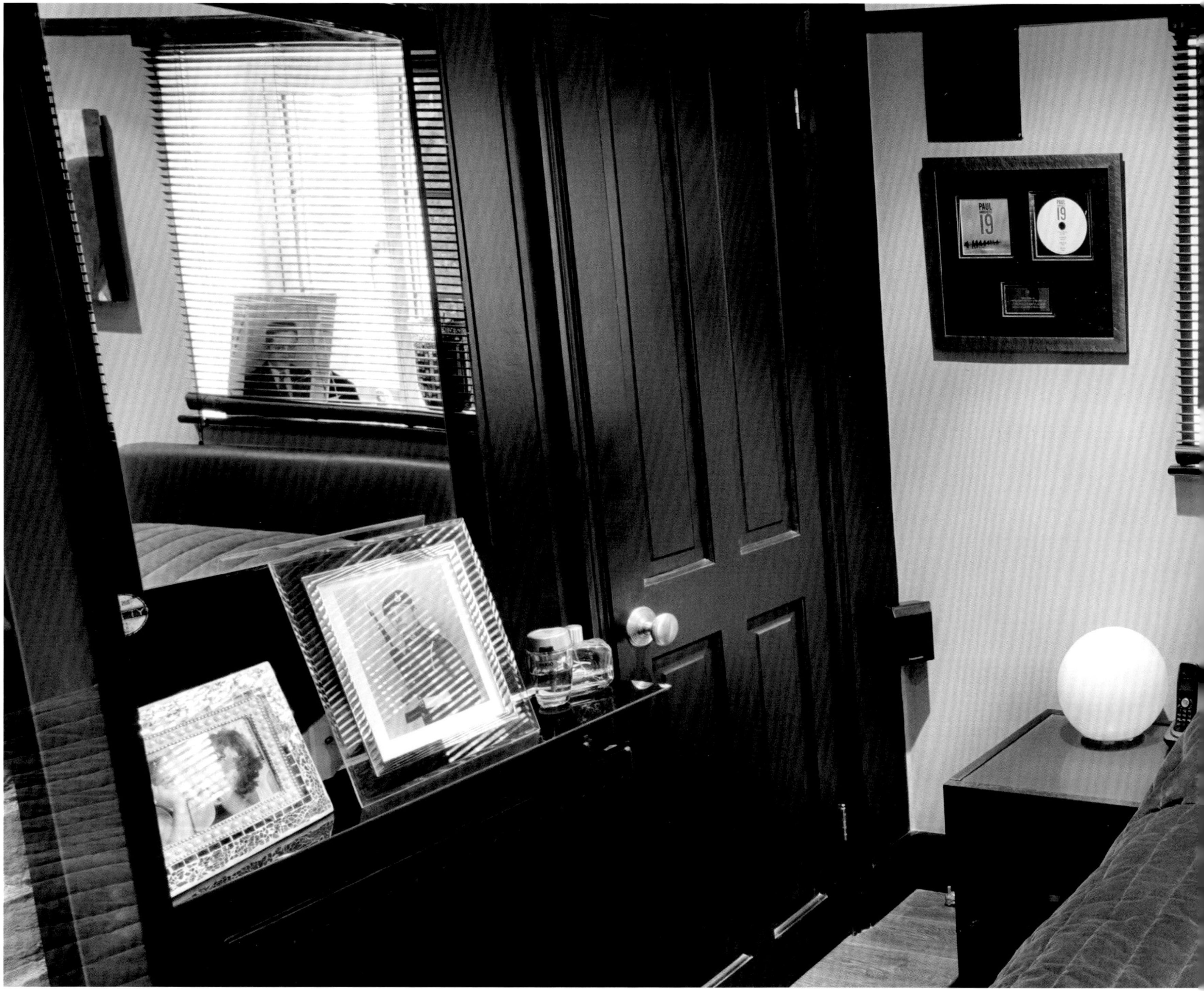

Royal Marine Commando Georgie Sparks, 19, was killed by small arms fire on November 27, 2008, in Helmand, Afghanistan. He was from Epping, Essex, England. His bedroom was photographed in March 2011.

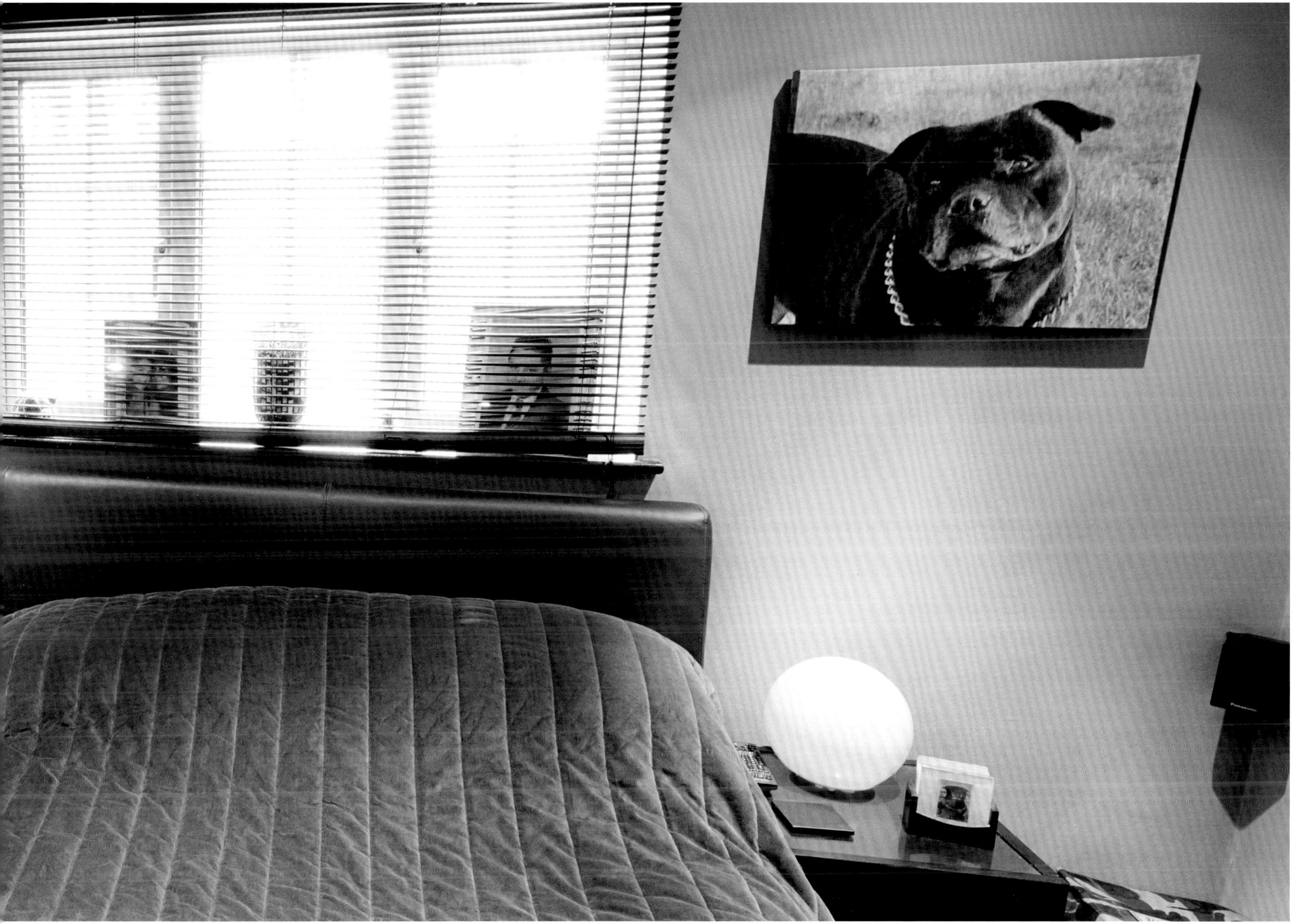

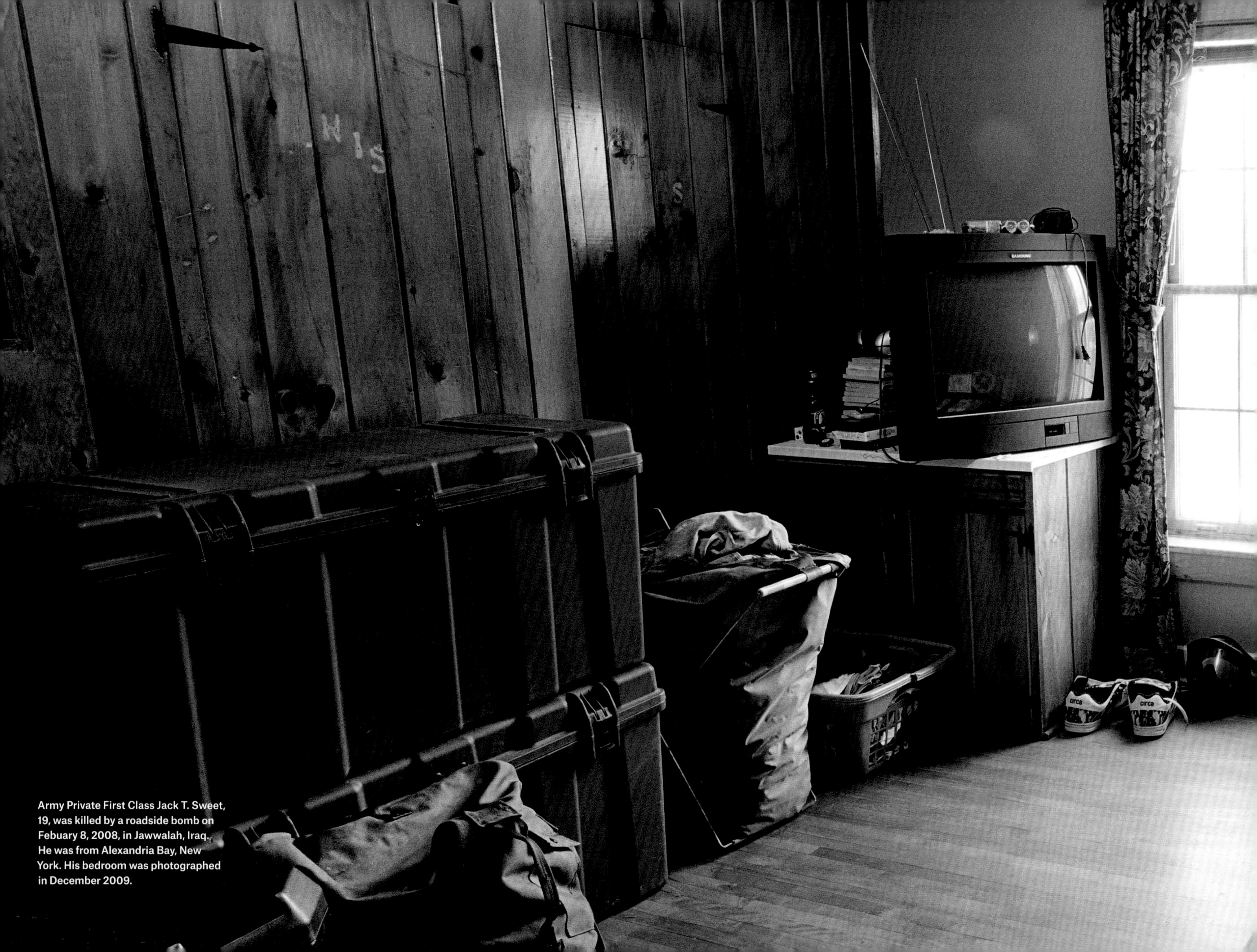

Army Private First Class Jack T. Sweet, 19, was killed by a roadside bomb on Febuary 8, 2008, in Jawwalah, Iraq. He was from Alexandria Bay, New York. His bedroom was photographed in December 2009.

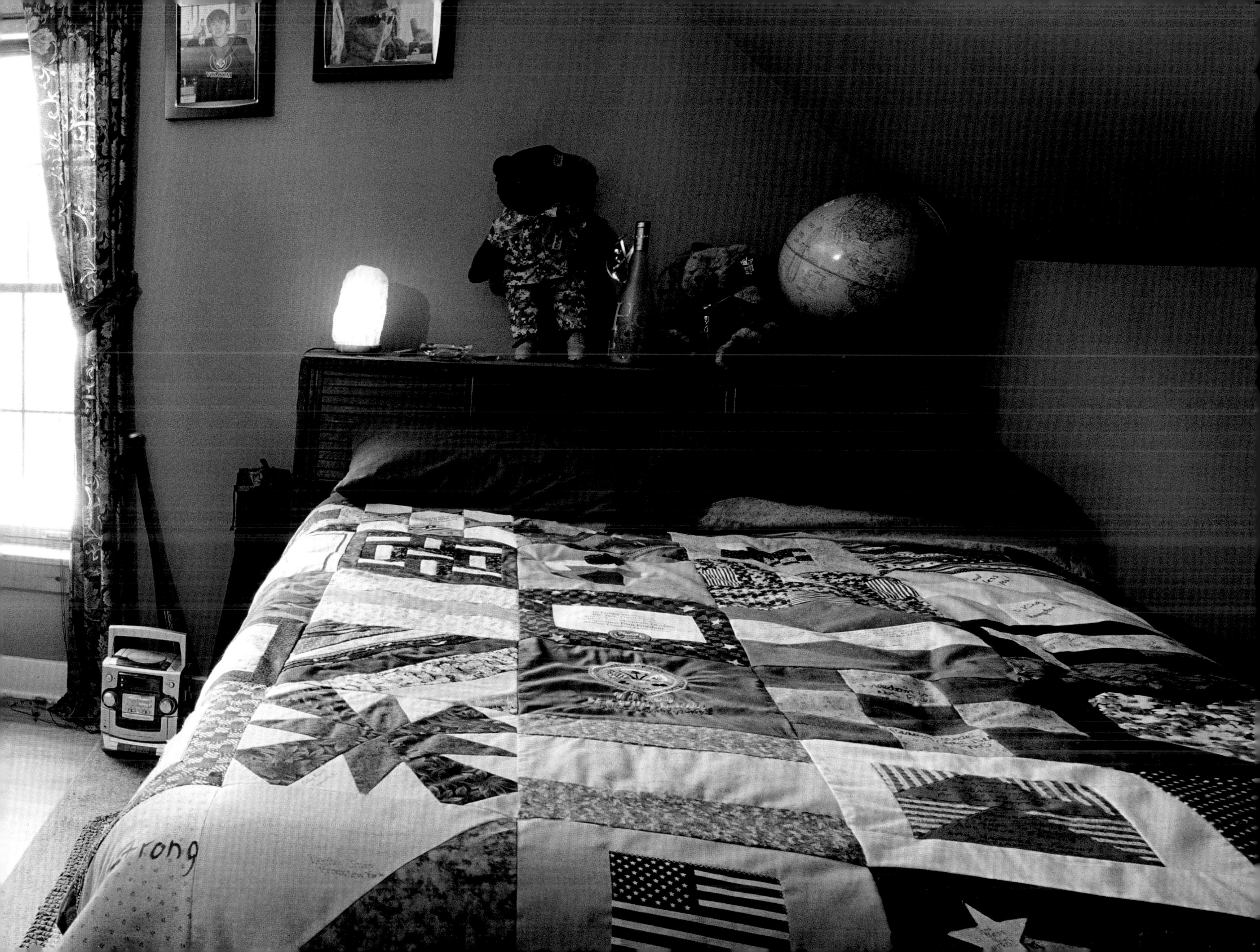

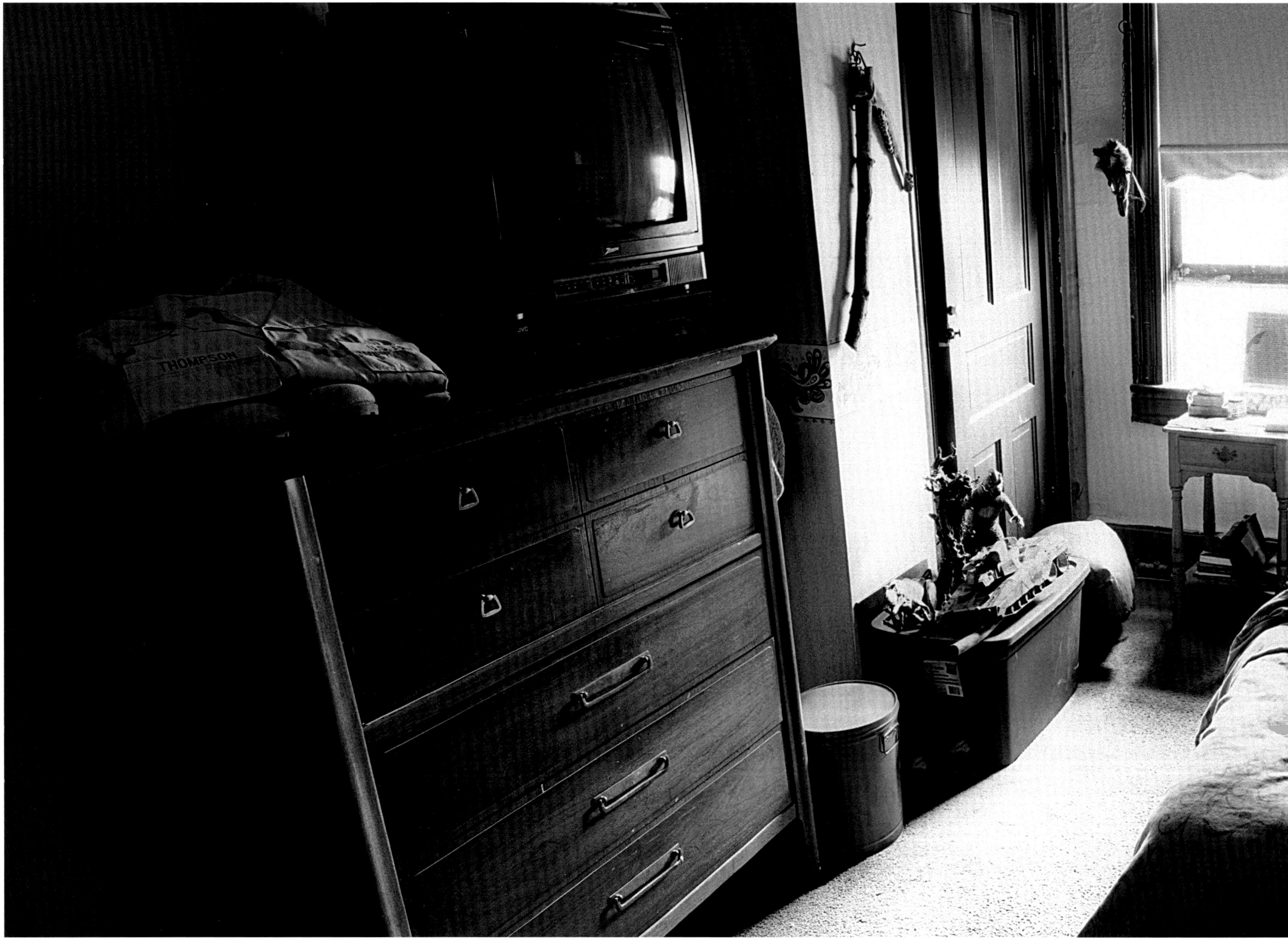
THOMPSON

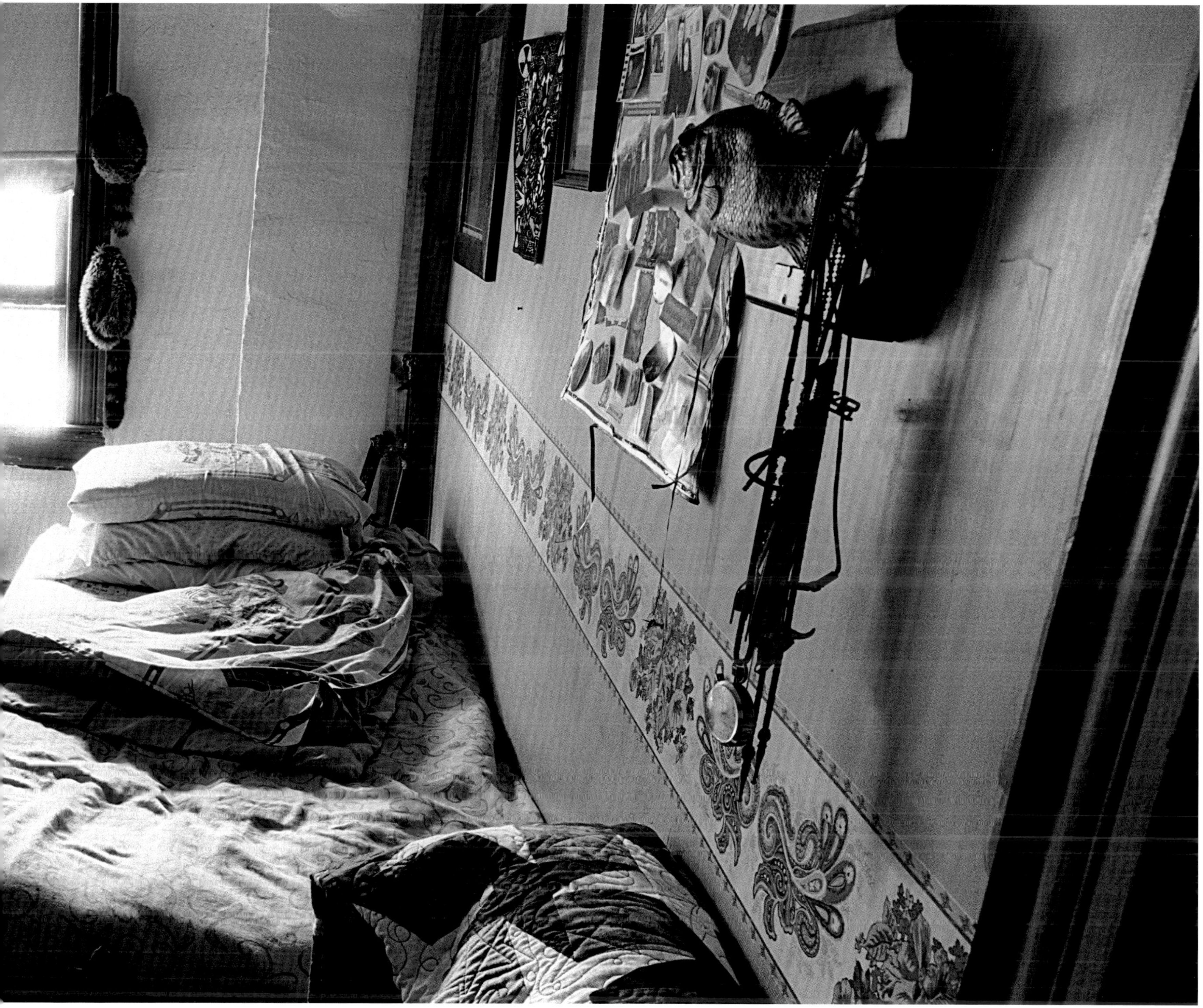

Army Private First Class Nils G. Thompson, 19, was killed by a sniper on August 4, 2005, in Mosul, Iraq. He was from Confluence, Pennsylvania. His bedroom was photographed in September 2007.

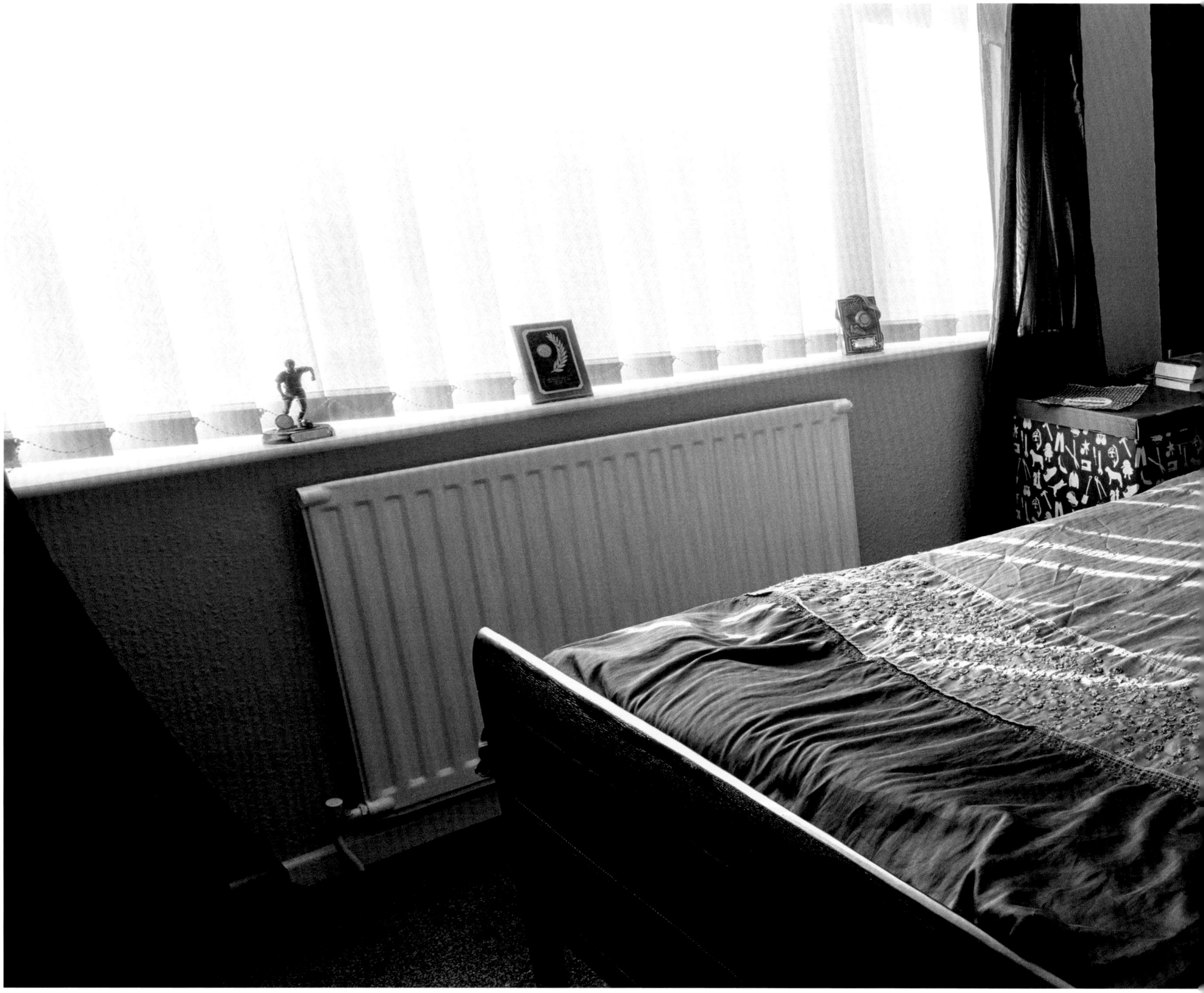

Sapper David Watson, 23, was killed by a roadside bomb on December 31, 2009, in Helmand, Afghanistan. He was from Wickham, Tyne and Wear, England. His bedroom was photographed in March 2011.

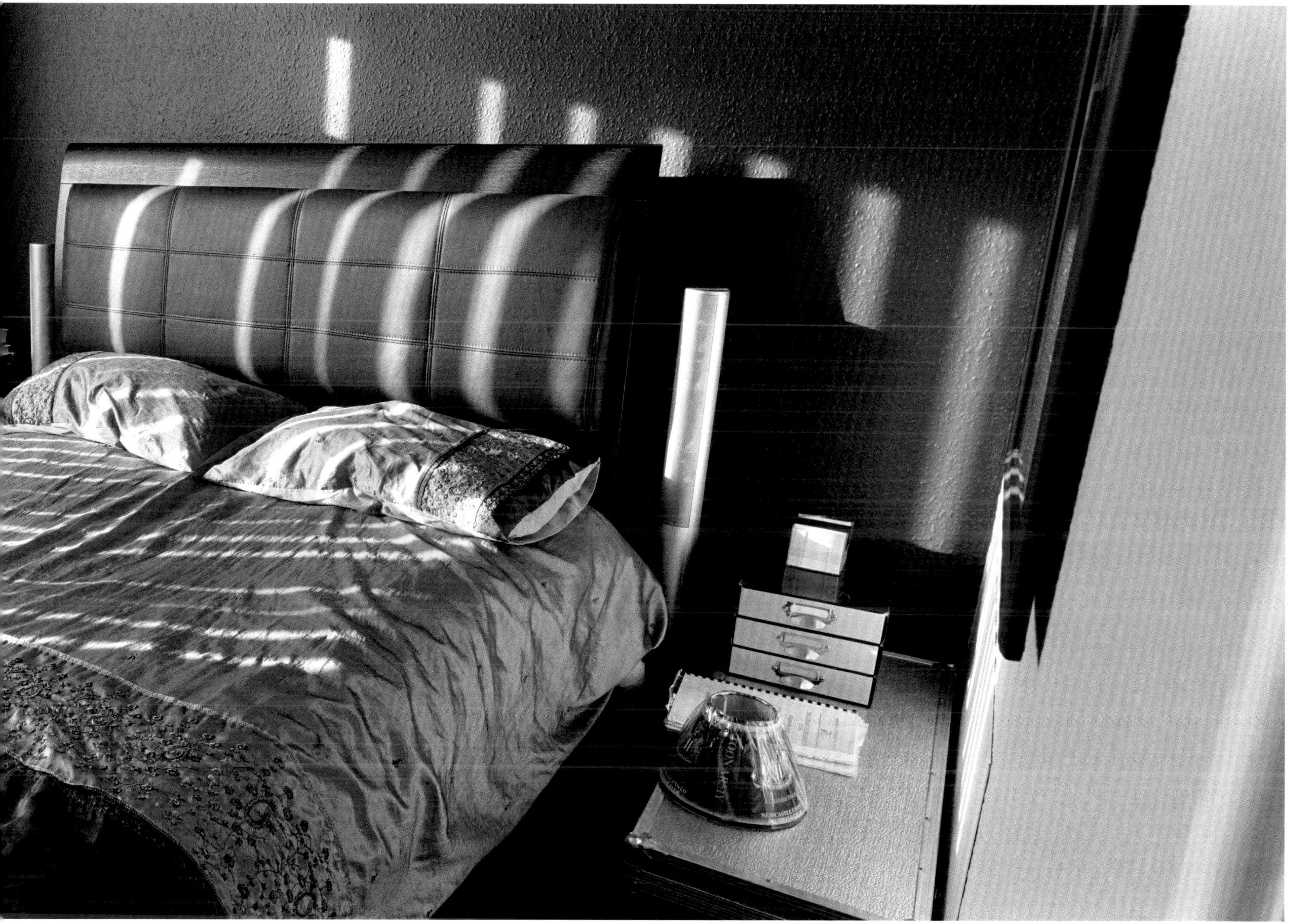

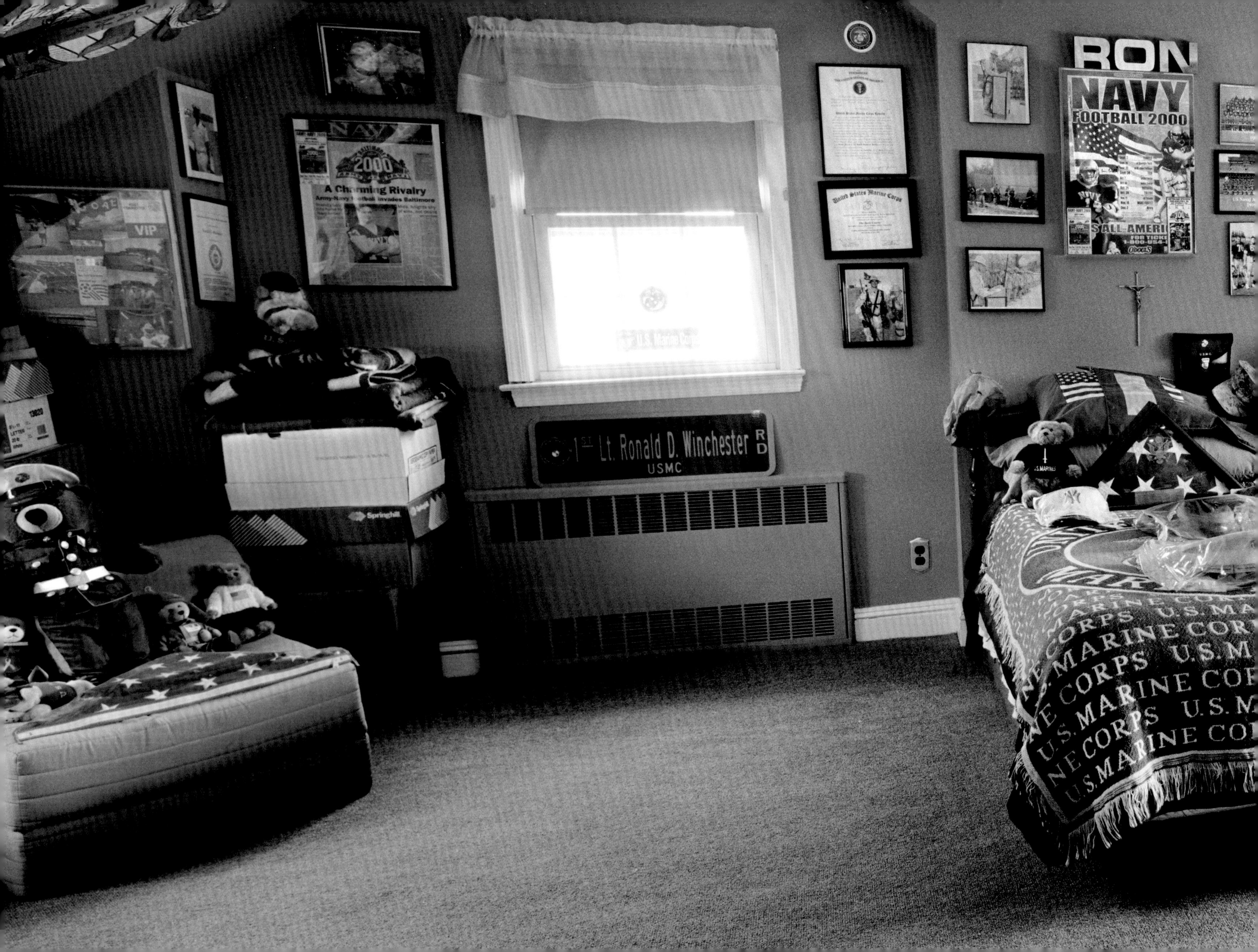
RON
NAVY
FOOTBALL 2000
2000
A Charming Rivalry
Army-Navy football invades Baltimore
VIP
United States Marine Corps
U.S. Marine Corps
1ST Lt. Ronald D. Winchester RD
USMC
Springhill
U.S. MARINES
U.S. MARINE CORPS

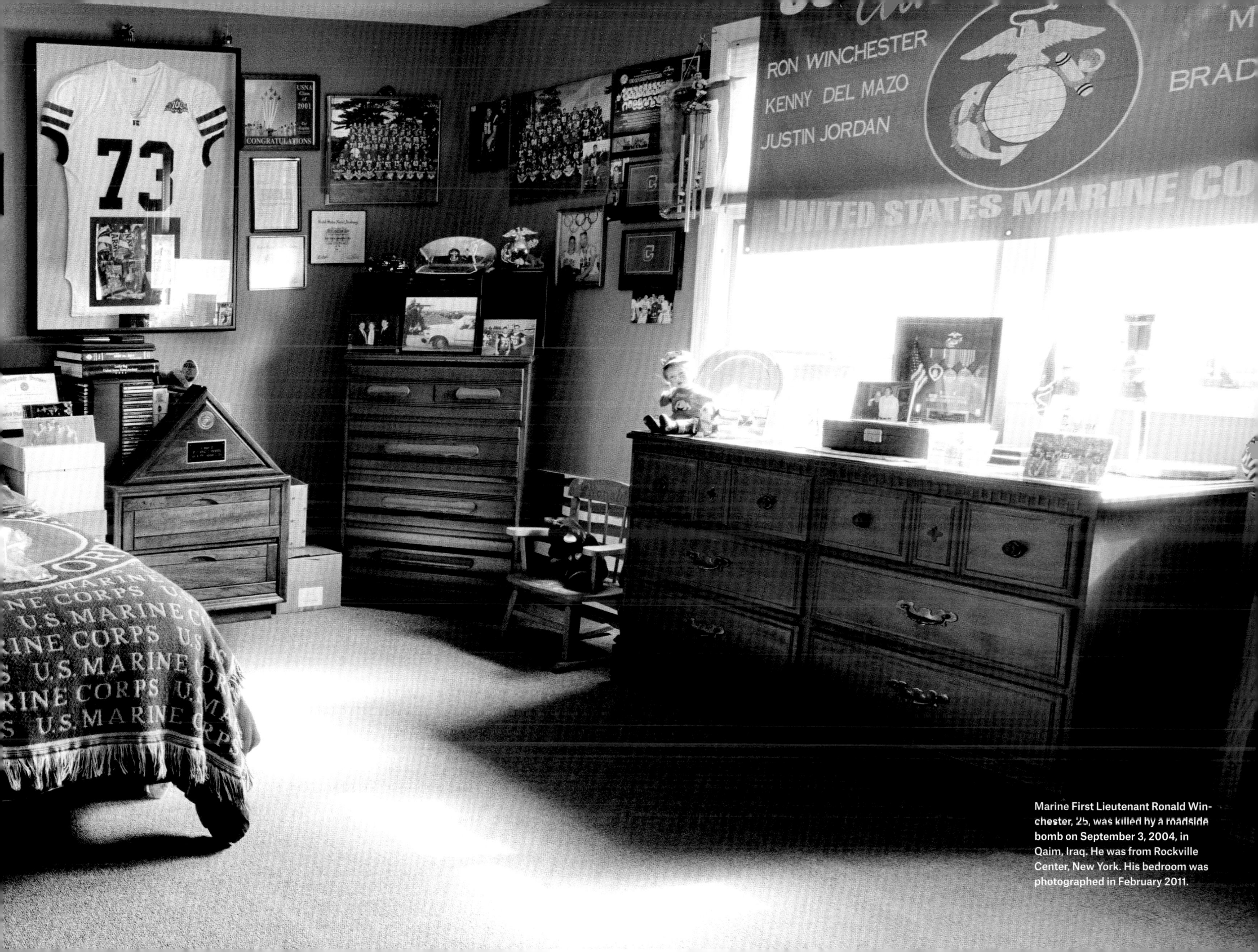

Marine First Lieutenant Ronald Winchester, 25, was killed by a roadside bomb on September 3, 2004, in Qaim, Iraq. He was from Rockville Center, New York. His bedroom was photographed in February 2011.

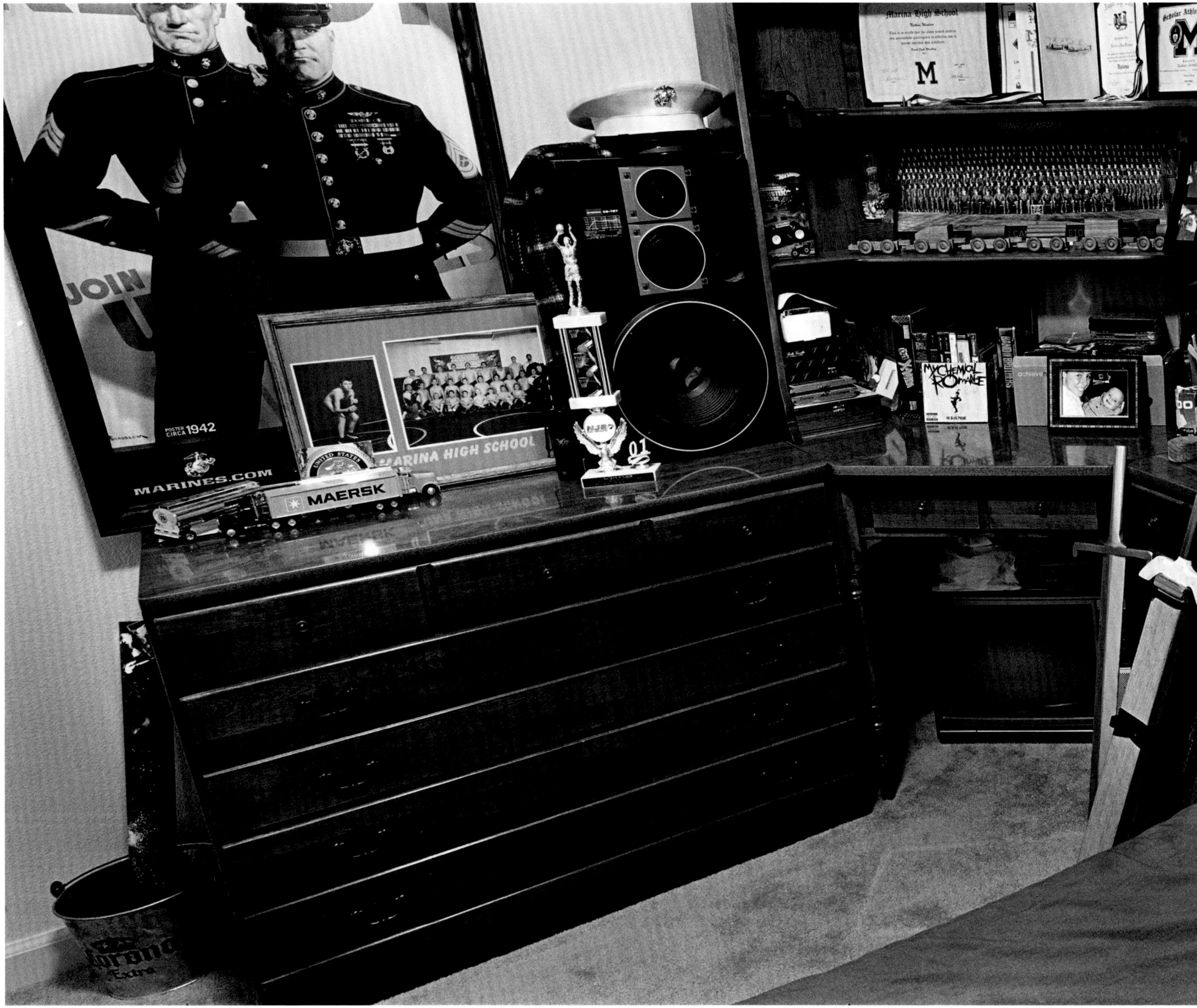

Marine Lance Corporal Nathanial D. Windsor, 20, was killed by a sniper on March 11, 2007, in Ramadi, Iraq. He was from Scappoose, Oregon. His bedroom was photographed in December 2009.

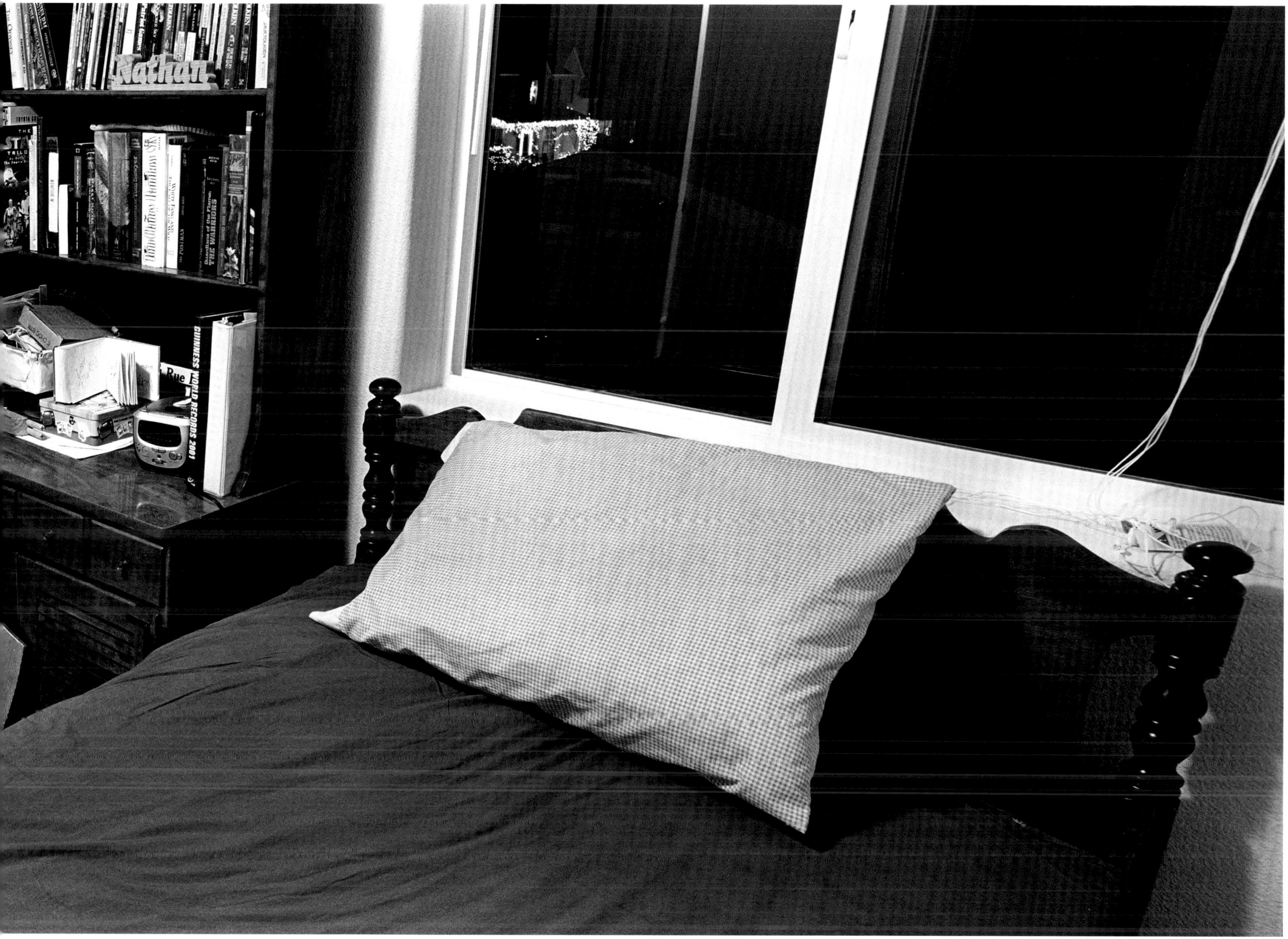
Nathan
GUINNESS WORLD RECORDS 2001

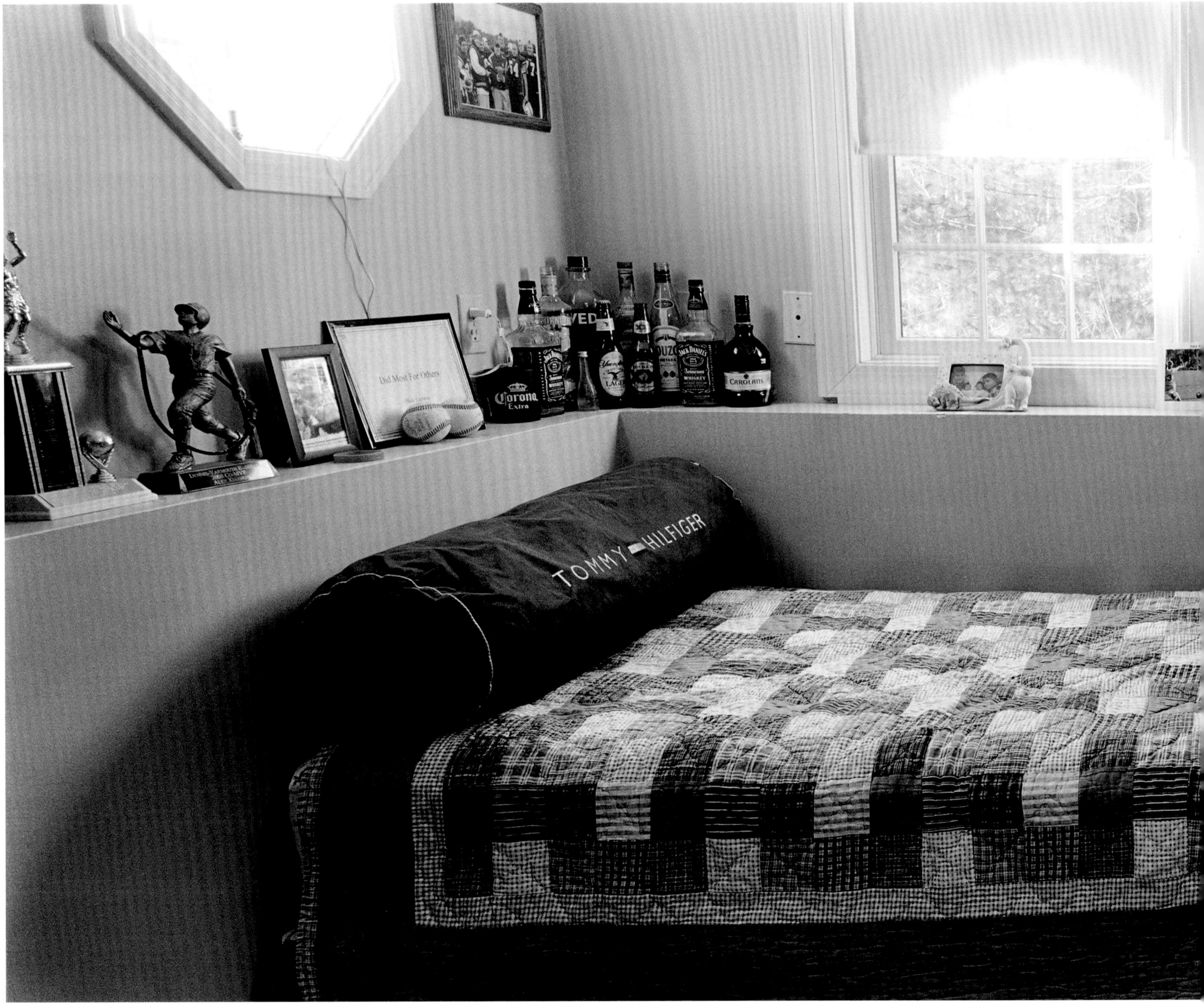

Marine Corporal Nicholas G. Xiarhos, 21, was killed in an IED attack on July 23, 2009, in the Garmsir district, Afghanistan. He was from Yarmouth Port, Massachusetts. His bedroom was photographed in January 2010.

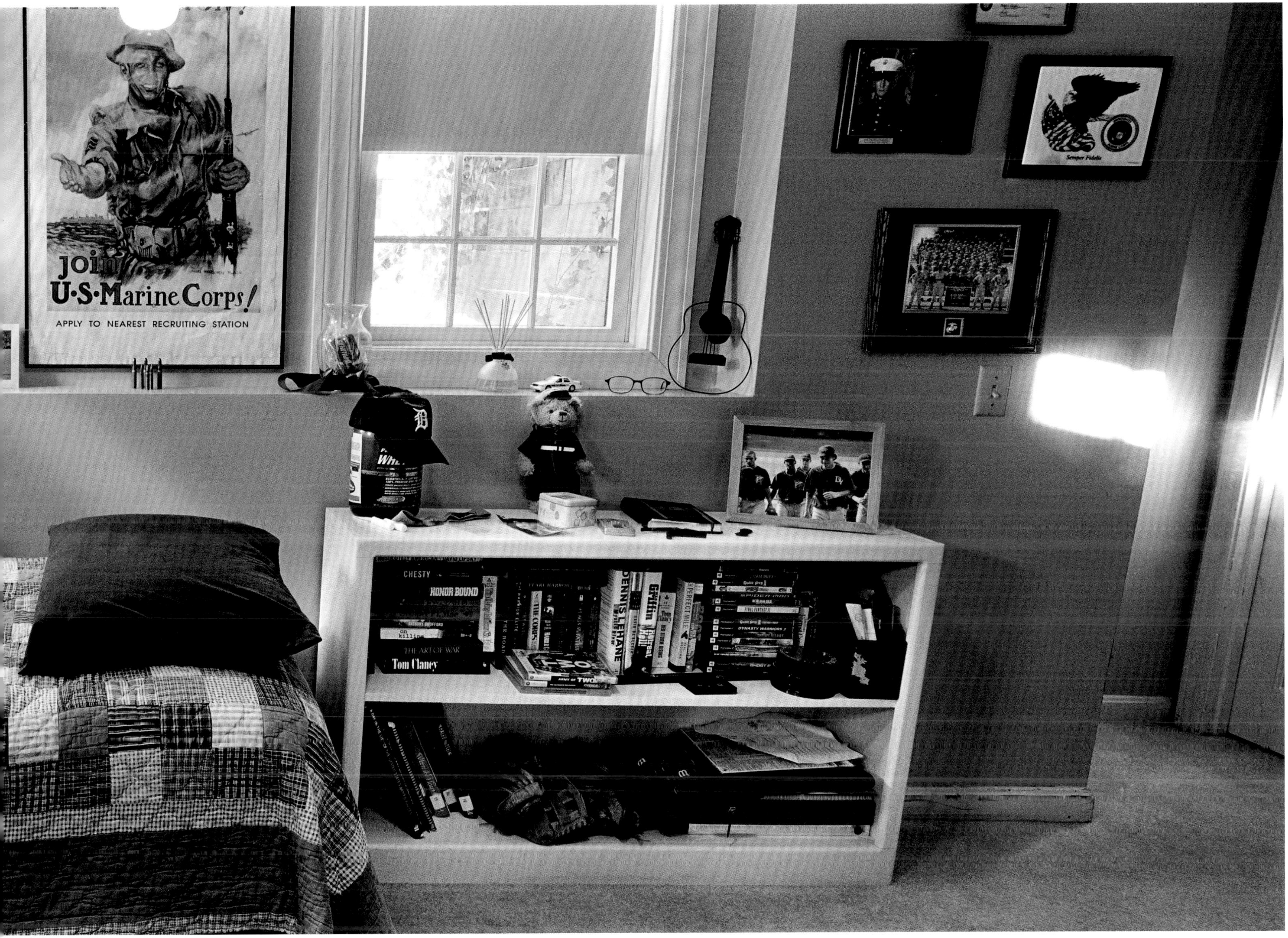
join
U·S·Marine Corps!
APPLY TO NEAREST RECRUITING STATION
CHESTY
HONOR BOUND
DENNIS LEHANE
THE ART OF WAR
Tom Clancy

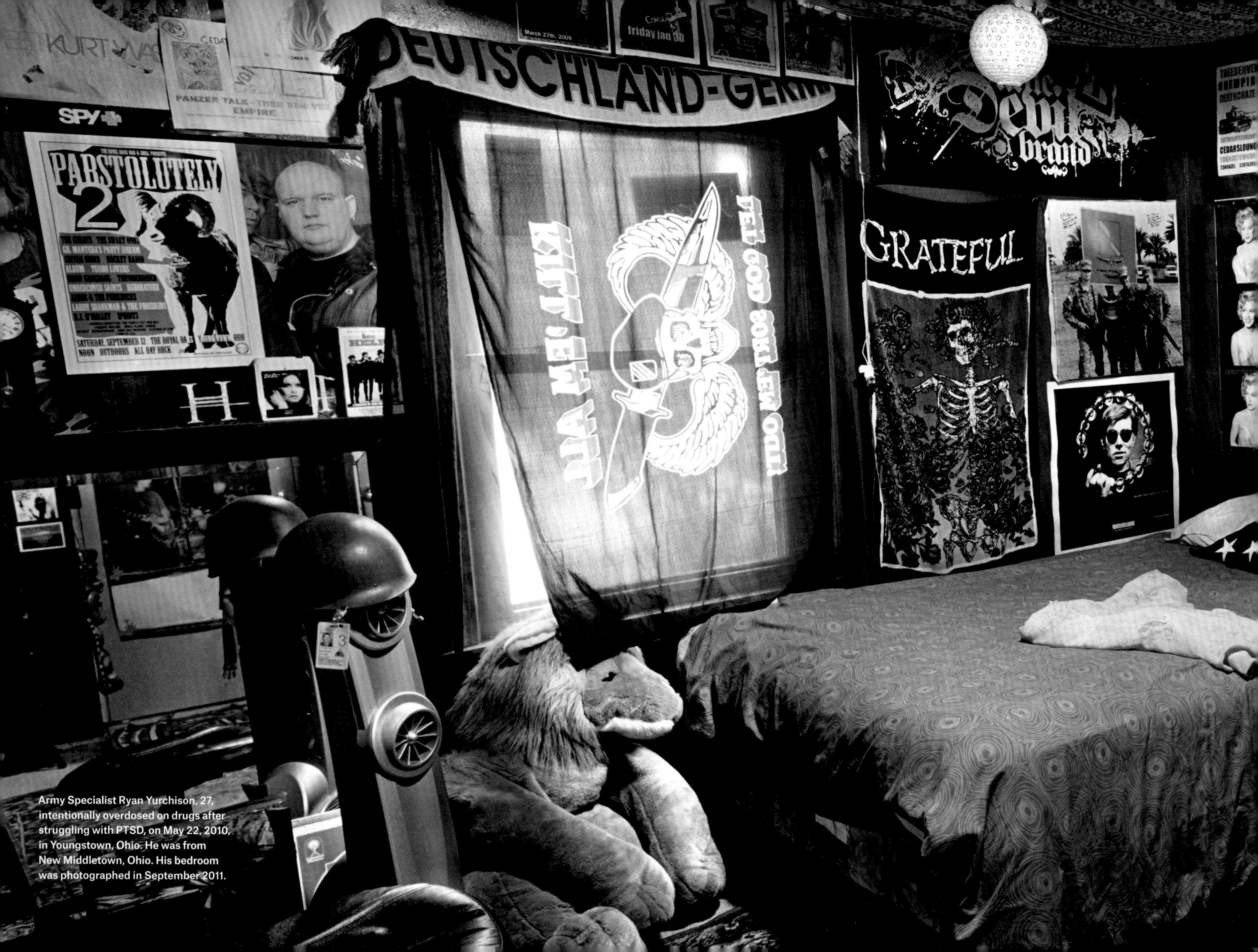

Army Specialist Ryan Yurchison, 27, intentionally overdosed on drugs after struggling with PTSD, on May 22, 2010, in Youngstown, Ohio. He was from New Middletown, Ohio. His bedroom was photographed in September 2011.

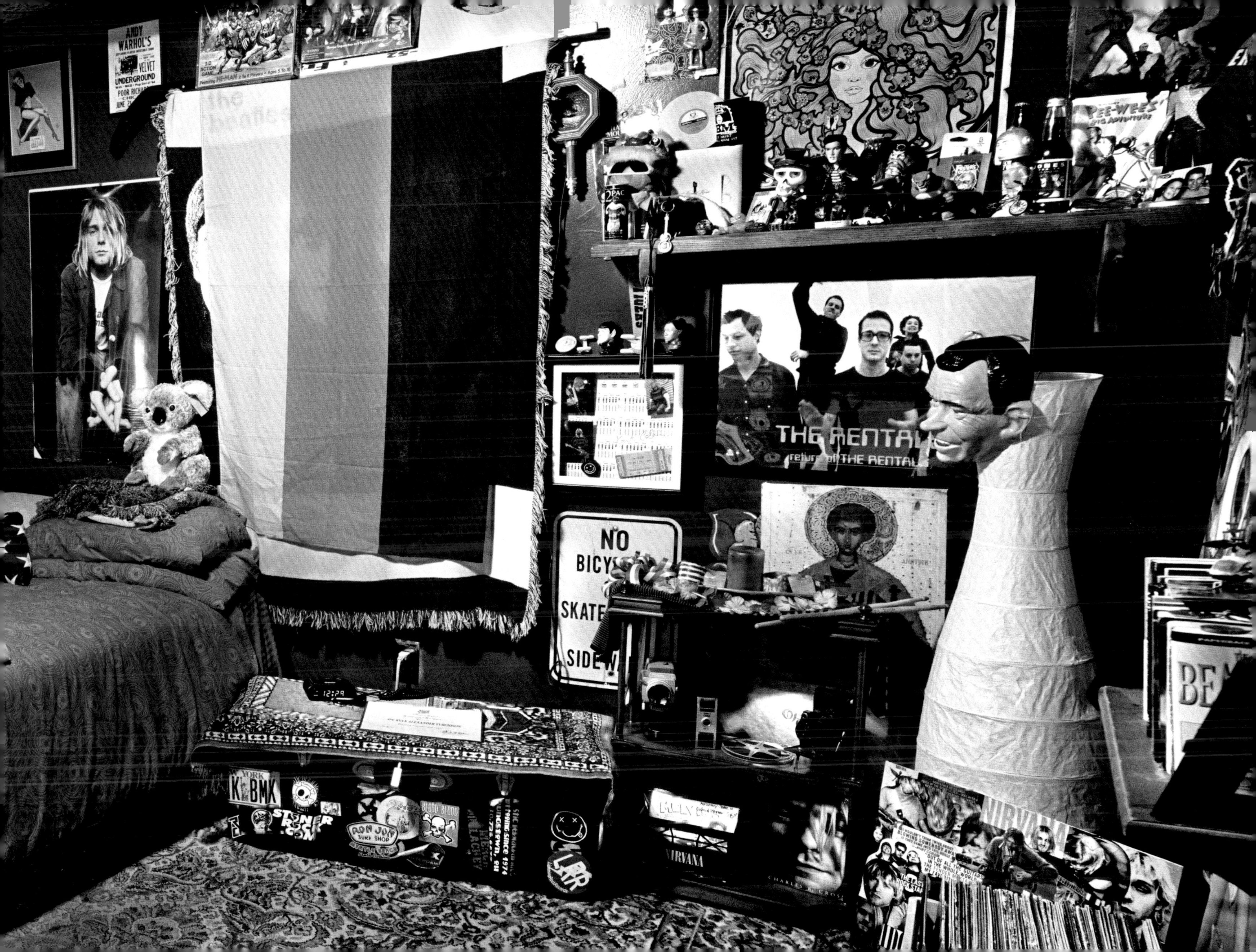
ANDY WARHOL'S
VELVET
UNDERGROUND
POOR RICHARD'S
the beatles
PEE-WEES'
THE RENTALS
return of THE RENTALS
NO
BICY
SKATE
SIDEW
NIRVANA
NIRVANA
RON JON SURF SHOP

ABSENCES

Ashley Gilbertson

On November 15, 2004, a week into an embed with a Marine company tearing through Falluja, I heard that an insurgent lay dead in a minaret from which he had been firing. No one had yet produced evidence that the insurgents were warring from mosques, which the Geneva Conventions put off-limits. I had to photograph him.

The company captain assigned a squad, including Lance Corporals William Miller and Christian Dominguez, to escort me, and soon I was climbing the stairs to the minaret behind them. Moments before we reached the top, Miller was shot point-blank by an enemy fighter. I ran out as fast as I could, covered in Miller's blood, forever changed.

I was too much in shock to photograph Miller being carried away, but if I had taken pictures, they would have depicted a crumpled, dying man. Those kinds of images show the horror and repugnance of war sure enough, and I've taken many of them. But they don't speak to the larger truth: war takes people away from those who love them. I came home. So did Dominguez. Billy Miller didn't. I needed to photograph his absence.

• • •

While I'd covered other conflicts, I focused on Iraq consistently from 2002. After six years, I was exhausted. I felt like I was trapped on one of those old slide carousels, projecting the same photos in constant rotation. Over time, the differences in my images diminished to subtleties only a trained eye would catch: Men in identical uniforms kicked in doors (again) and looked tired (still) and chain-smoked between raids. Civilians continued to be terrified and broke down when they lost a relative to a bullet or a bomb. One cadaver was indistinguishable from the next, and worse still, they'd ceased to shock me.

Every time I returned to Iraq, which since 2003 I'd been doing on contract for the *New York Times*, I exercised the same old muscles and rarely altered my approach. It made sense: access and safety are the conflict photographer's ultimate challenge; when the threat of kidnapping or car bombs colors each moment, it's difficult to think of a novel or alternative approach. If you have access, you get in and make the photograph.

There are a few photographers whose approach to war photography has evolved. And certainly they produce powerful essays that can engage audiences on new levels. But for the most part, I haven't seen much change since the advent of the 35-millimeter camera in 1934. Conflict photography is still important, and I admire those who go to the frontlines and collect evidence, document history. I question, however, how much our readers pay attention. Simon Norfolk, a photographer who has spent a decade working war zones in large format, and who displays his work in museums and galleries, is even more critical. In a video for the Tate Modern, he refers to news images being produced in Afghanistan as "work that is pouring out, like some kind of sewer pipe with a crack in the side of it, which is the billion-pictures-per-hour of modern photojournalism."

I was inspired as a teenager by photographs of the Vietnam war, Robert Capa's stories, and biographies of World War II correspondents. Above all, I respected—revered, even—the role of the photographer as witness, an impartial chronicler on the front lines of history. As I worked through Iraq over the years, I thought of images by photographers like Mathew Brady, David Douglas Duncan, Capa, and James Nachtwey, and the impact they had made. But things had changed; war photography would never be the same. I was the next generation of photographer trying to act like one from a previous era.

At some point in history, we were able to stand aside and simply bear witness. Today, like it or not, we are seen as players on the battlefield, and on some of the more carefully managed press events, it feels like we're actors, manipulated by directors who remain unseen. Propaganda campaigns remain as important as battles themselves, and media dossiers compiled by the Rendon Group for the U.S. military—classifying reporters' dispatches as "positive," "negative," or "neutral"—remove any doubts about our role in these productions. We contribute to the war machine, no matter our intentions. The best analogy came from an artist I knew back in my native Australia. He told me he'd been rethinking the chessboard, and planned on replacing the traditional pieces with updated versions. His set would include a war correspondent.

As I came to understand my position on the battlefield, I was forced to rethink my role. If I wasn't witness, what was I? I had tired of seeing these scenes, and I felt readers were fatigued too. I became certain of one thing: I was failing in my role as a conflict photographer.

In 2008 I returned from a trip to Iraq, convinced it would be my last. I couldn't bring myself to return. But conflict is one of the most interesting aspects of humanity, and though I didn't want to return, I couldn't feign interest in anything other than war.

The one aspect of the wars in Afghanistan and Iraq that had failed to receive enough coverage, I thought, was the deaths of American soldiers and Marines. I started visiting Arlington National Cemetery. I spent almost a month at Section 60, the parcel of land reserved for those killed in Iraq and Afghanistan. I would arrive early each morning, when the cemetery was still deserted, and sit under a tree and wait.

I joined families having picnics on their child's plot. I talked to girlfriends and wives who had come to lie atop the fresh sod covering their loved one's corpse, or at least what was left of it. Battle buddies often arrived, though they didn't talk much. Silence seemed to stand in for an unspoken sense of responsibility. Those guys usually took a knee, placed one hand on the headstone, and bowed their heads, eyes tightly closed. When they finished, they would stand and leave, trying not to make eye contact with other mourners.

I met a man named Tom Gugliuzza-Smith, who would visit every day to read to the dead and help keep their graves in order. He hadn't lost a son, but he liked visiting on behalf of families who lived too far away to come regularly.

My time at Arlington gave me access to a tiny minority of Americans: those directly touched by the wars in Iraq and Afghanistan. These families had borne the brunt of the nation's war on terror, yet they wept quietly, alone, here and in towns across America. Their lives were lived far from reporters, opinion columnists, and television studios. These families struck me as more isolated in their grief than any other community I've photographed. They lived every day with a tragic reality few pundits or politicians would come near: their dead sons and daughters, brothers and sisters.

"People see it on the evening news, and forget it by Letterman," said a mother at Arlington. She was explaining how she felt the country mourned its lost citizens. And that was in 2007, when the names of the dead were still regularly reported on television news. The networks stopped the practice soon after.

She expressed how I was feeling perfectly. A soldier dies. Next of kin are notified. The Pentagon releases the name to the press. In some small town, a local reporter knocks on the door of a bereaved family's home and asks for comment. A boilerplate obituary appears in the next day's paper with a soulless military headshot: John Doe, from Springfield, liked Monday Night Football and seeing movies with friends. Soon enough, readers stop paying attention. They stop for the same reason they turn away from images of war itself. They've seen it before. The same thing over and over.

On many mornings at Arlington, I'd arrive to find a backhoe finishing its work, opening a fresh plot for a funeral later that day. The military invites the press to cover burials if the family permits it. At those events, photographers are kept in a pen about two hundred yards from the burial site. Here, in death's most intimate setting, we capture emotion only with a telephoto lens. The frames are as intimate as sports photographs, footballs replaced by folded American flags, cheering fans by weeping families.

I soon realized that in order to show the heartbreak of the soldiers' parents, siblings, spouses, and children, I needed to contact the families directly and find some other way to document these losses.

Tommy Gilbert was a twenty-four-year-old Marine sergeant who was killed by an improvised explosive device in Falluja, Iraq. I learned that his parents were arranging a memorial service for him at their home in Downers Grove, Illinois, a suburb of Chicago. They had invited Tommy's comrades, who'd just returned from their deployment. Tommy parents were distraught when I spoke to them on the phone from New York, but they invited me to attend the service. I was surprised that they consented to let me photograph Tommy's memorial, but downright floored when they greeted me with hugs, as if I were family. The photographs I made that day weren't published, but the Gilberts' embrace had opened the door to a closer look at how fallen servicemen were being remembered at home.

A few months later, I was at home with my wife, Joanna, sitting in our office. We were looking over a photo spread the *New York Times* had run to commemorate yet another casualty milestone for the wars in Iraq and Afganistan. Two full pages showed a solemn grid of head shots, hundreds and hundreds of official portraits of uniformed—and somewhat uniform—soldiers and marines who had been killed. Joanna was frustrated, she said, that the media only ever presented these fallen men and women as soldiers, never as people with families and friends and lives outside of war, lives with which those of us not directly effected by war could identify. "You need to humanize them, to show us that they were people first, kids even, before they were soldiers," she said. "What's left? Their families, but that's not them. Their bedrooms. You need to photograph their bedrooms."

• • •

When we lived with our parents, most of us had a bedroom to ourselves. Our bedroom was the space we took ownership of, and in it we placed the things we loved most, reminders of what we longed for and aspired to. It was a place to which we could retreat from the world and feel protected. There we could express ourselves without judgment, and only our mothers could make us clean it.

One of the first bedrooms I photographed belonged to Zachary Clouser, who was nineteen years old when he was killed by a roadside bomb in Baghdad. His mother, Deb, had taken me into her son's room, and we stood there as she talked about Zach's life. Trophies lined the windowsill, and the caption on a framed picture of a young Zach wearing a goofy grin read "Most Valuable Player." Zach had thrown the winning pitch in his team's championship game in 1998.

Zach's mom said academics weren't his strong suit. Zach's stepfather, Ron, recalled dropping him off at school and idling in the car outside to make sure he entered the building. One time Zach turned and walked the other way, only to have Ron pull up beside him and say, "Where do you think you're goin'? School's that way." Deb remembered wanting to go into the school herself so she could sit behind her son and smack him on the back of the head when he tried to go to sleep.

Composing a frame in Zach's bedroom, I felt, for the first time in ten years of covering battles and uprisings, that I was photographing war. The tragedy and the finality of this space was, to my heart, a more telling and honest explanation of what I had witnessed in Iraq than the countless photographs I had made there. The exploding bombs, morgues overflowing with corpses, and wounded soldiers being loaded onto helicopters were thousands of miles away. But in bedrooms like this, it felt like the conflicts were just outside, pressing against the walls.

Inside Zach's room, and every other room in this book, I often had the sense that the former occupant was about to walk in and tell me to get out. I felt like a trespasser, and I thought about what they would make of the work. Before entering a room I took off my shoes, and once inside I was very cautious not to touch anything. I'd force myself and my tripod into ridiculous positions to avoid contact with so much as the corner of a bed or a closet door.

The objects I found in these forty bedrooms represent milestones of shortened lives: a framed diploma, photos from prom, a copy of the Constitution from a class trip to Washington, an animal jaw tied to a branch—a souvenir from a family trip to Yellowstone. There were also things that hinted at the occupant's purpose: a Bin Laden "wanted" poster, a page torn from *Time* magazine's 9/11 issue showing James Nachtwey's photograph of the smoldering Twin Towers. It was these objects that compelled me to shoot with black-and-white film. I wanted to present them neutrally, without the distraction of color, so that the viewer could digest as much of the detail as possible.

I also decided to use a panoramic camera and an extreme wide-angle lens. This allowed me to include almost half of a room in a single image. The expansive format suited the shape of the beds, the central subject in most of the images and the link between every room.

Initially, the project concerned only Americans killed in Iraq, largely due to my experience working with U.S. forces there and, more personally, my struggle with Billy Miller's death in 2004. However, as I became more deeply immersed in the work, as my time in Iraq grew distant, and as more troops were killed in Afghanistan, the project expanded.

In 2010 I was invited to show the photographs at a museum in Amsterdam. I was concerned that a European audience would dismiss the project as a purely American issue. With encouragement from the curators, Marla Ulrich and Eric Kessels, I decided to photograph two Dutch servicemen's rooms for the show. The response to the exhibition was very positive. The inclusion of the Dutch rooms gave museum-goers a connection to the wars' consequence on both local and universal levels. Today, this book also contains bedrooms belonging to troops from Canada, England, France, Germany, Italy, and Scotland, each of which sent significant numbers of their citizens to Iraq or Afghanistan.

In selecting rooms to photograph, I applied certain criteria. Most importantly, a room needed to be intact, as the owner left it. I decided I couldn't include rooms that had been converted into offices or taken over by siblings. Some of the rooms I photographed had been altered slightly, usually with small additions made. Quite a few rooms had large black plastic trunks containing the soldier's possessions, shipped home from wherever they were killed. The items inside were painstakingly catalogued and packed, usually by a friend, just hours after the death. Many families I met couldn't open these trunks, so they just sat in the bedroom, padlocked, like time capsules within time capsules.

In Jack Sweet's bedroom, two of those trunks were stacked by a hamper filled with dirty clothes. He'd been dead two years, and the clothes still smelled like him. His father, Glenn, said he still hoped his son would come home and do his laundry. Many parents told me that the moment they realized they'd forgotten their child's smell was one of the hardest milestones of their loss. Their memory of the child's voice, they'd tell me, was the next to fade. Videos are treasured for that reason, and every so often I met parents who kept their son's mobile phone connected; they would call and listen to his voicemail greeting. Some parents regularly called their child's phone to leave messages; then, when the mailbox was filled up, they would have to delete them all to make room for more.

Uniforms were sometimes added to the rooms too. Along with the trunks, the uniforms are sent to the family by the military, neatly folded and carefully stacked, name patches facing out. Some families hang the uniform, as though their child might come home at any moment and need it ready for an event.

In the U.S. bedrooms, American flags were popular. Many had been nailed to walls and ceilings by the kids themselves. After they've died, though, a second flag often appears somewhere. This flag has been folded twelve times with precision and ceremony by six honor guards at a military funeral. Each fold carries a symbolic meaning, the ninth and tenth being tributes to motherhood and fatherhood.

Brandon Craig was from Earleville, Maryland, a tiny farming town where, before meeting his parents, I had coffee and watched local kids pass time chasing chickens around gas pumps. His father, Danny, is a mechanic who works on heavy machinery for the local community. He was stoic when I talked to him and his wife at their home. We entered his son's room together, and I asked about two wrapped Christmas presents stacked on top of a chest of drawers.

Danny told me that one Christmas, after Brandon had turned eighteen, his son had jokingly complained that he no longer received toys, "Somethin' to play with!" he'd said. So Danny began a family tradition, buying his adult children toys every Christmas. Two Christmases had passed since Brandon had died, and the two presents were from his dad, lovingly wrapped, his son's name carefully inscribed on the paper.

Some items, I came to learn, are commonly removed by troops before they deploy. In spring 2011, I was invited to show the photographs and lecture at Indiana University South Bend. I spoke to a class that included several veterans among the students. One of them explained that before deploying, he and his friends had gone through their own bedrooms, or "rat-holes," as he called them, and removed "sensitive" items. They didn't want to die downrange and have their parents find them.

• • •

The project of photographing the bedrooms depended entirely on trust. Exposing the photograph itself was comparatively simple—there were only so many angles I could find in these small spaces. What took time was finding the families, making contact, and sitting and talking with them, in some cases for a couple of hours and in others for days over several trips, until they were comfortable with the project. In those conversations, I did my best to explain the concept of the work and to learn as much as I could about the soldier or Marine.

The first room that I photographed belonged to Tommy Gilbert, the Marine sergeant killed in Falluja whose parents had invited me to photograph his memorial service. After that first visit, I returned to Downers Grove, Illinois, to meet more of Tommy's friends and family and to see some of his neighborhood haunts. I had dinner one night with his parents, Michael and Terri, in a pub they used to frequent as a family. Another night I drank at a nearby bar where Tommy used to put back Irish Car Bombs with friends and Macallan single malts if his dad was buying.

His parents talked about their son and the moments they'd shared with him. The day when, still a boy, he'd covered himself head to toe in cicadas; or his love of playing gin rummy with his father. In conversations like these, with the hundreds of other families I'd meet or speak to by telephone over the next four years, we'd talk about the pain of losing a child. I've heard people say it's the most traumatic event a human being can experience, and if these conversations are an indication, I'd have to agree.

I'd regularly hear variations on the same experiences: The moment the uniformed service member came to the door bearing news of the death. The feeling of a thousand-pound weight bearing down on a parent, lasting for months, making it near impossible to get out of bed. The faint hope that there'd been a mistake or that their child was on a secret mission and could actually walk through the door at any moment. The contemplation of suicide. One mother, whose son had killed himself, told me of her trip to Walmart to buy bullets so she could join him in heaven.

Every cherished memory was shadowed by the knowledge that the happiness could never be relived. "We'd daydream together," said Tommy's dad, Michael, "but now I have no one to daydream with."

Photographing these spaces carried a responsibility. I quickly came to understand that after death, all that's left are memories. To trust somebody, an outsider, with any of those memories requires an enormous leap of faith.

After that first room, I began trying to locate families by sorting through a *Washington Post* website called *Faces of the Fallen*. There I could search by age, state, and hometown. Often there would be links to obituaries that had appeared in local papers. I took into consideration factors suggesting that an intact room might still exist. Younger troops were more likely to be living at home, and I didn't phone families of those who had been married. Spaces shared with spouses were not, rightly or wrongly, within the scope of the project.

After I'd gathered basic information, I turned to the white pages, with limited success. When that didn't work, Facebook was helpful. There, it was simple to locate family and write messages, though often I received no response. Sometimes there were memorials online, and I would contact the page's administrator. Occasionally, a family had no Internet access, like Karina Lau's parents in Livingston, California, so I sent them letters.

Karina was killed when her helicopter crashed near Falluja on November 2, 2003. I met her parents, Ruth and Augustin Lau, at their home in December 2009. Karina's room was still perfectly intact, preserved behind a locked door off the foyer.

Karina was of mixed heritage, born to a Chinese father and a Mexican mother. Her hometown, two hours inland from San Francisco, was tiny and inhabited almost entirely by migrant laborers. I was told she had dreamed of great things. She was infatuated by everything musical. She played several instruments, she sang. In her room there were dozens of VHS tapes of old Hollywood musicals. When she graduated from the local high school, she received a four-year music scholarship to the nearby University of the Pacific.

She hated it. As much as she loved class, she couldn't bear her roommates and the constant drinking and parties. She returned home, depressed and unsure of her future. When the recruiter called, Ruth told me, Karina was at her most vulnerable. Ruth picked up the phone, and a man asked for Karina, who was watching television on the couch. Ruth passed her the receiver.

We went through family photo albums, and when Ruth came upon the pictures of her daughter's funeral, she began rubbing the glossy surface of a photo of a muscular African-American pallbearer. "Him," she said quietly, almost to herself. "He's the one who called."

She regrets passing the phone to her daughter that day. "Maybe if I hadn't," she said, "Karina would be here."

Most parents were understandably cautious when I first called. I had many conversations that were almost entirely one-sided—me on the phone explaining what the project was, who I was, why I wanted to do this. I would follow up with an e-mail, I'd tell them, showing examples of the work, photographs of other bedrooms. I'd ask that both parents read the e-mail before we spoke again, when hopefully we would schedule a time to meet.

It was important that both parents agree to participate. If either of them was not entirely comfortable with the idea, I wouldn't shoot. It was early in the project when I first had to navigate this issue.

Nils Thompson was a nineteen-year-old who lived on a farm on the outskirts of Confluence, a very small town in southwest Pennsylvania. I spent hours over a few different trips there, sitting on the porch with his mother, Frances, overlooking the only road leading through town—the same road that she'd been looking at in August 2005, when a car driven by a single soldier in dress uniform pulled up to inform her that Nils had been shot dead by a sniper in Mosul, Iraq.

"Are you Ms. Frances Thompson? Are you the mother of Private First Class Nils G. Thompson?

"The Secretary of the Army has asked me to express his deep regret that your son . . ."

Frances told me she had given up drinking iced coffee as penance, hoping God would protect her son when he went to Iraq. When Nils called her from Mosul, he told his mother that every day when he drank his iced coffee, he'd think of her. He said in it a peculiar way, and Frances realized he was desperate for a connection to her and to his home. She started drinking it again, to share the experience with her son thousands of miles away. "It was like our shared prayer time," she said. "I still prayed, of course. 'God,' I'd say, 'please protect my Nilsie.'"

Frances smiled when she recalled tapping the maple trees that grew wild on their property. The family cooked it down over their fireplace, and the process filled the house with a rich, sweet smell. Before it turned into syrup, the family would drink it. "We called it maple tea," she said.

Although Frances was receptive, Nils's father, also named Nils, wasn't sure he wanted his son's room in the project. He was concerned about the potential politicization of his son's death. I found out when I arrived that some mornings he would go into his son's room and begin dismantling it. When he was out, Frances would put things back in their place.

On my third visit with them, Nils's father came home late one night. I was staying at the house, and we sat in front of the fireplace and talked about his son. He showed me the casualty report he'd gotten from the army, cataloguing every grim detail of his son's death. He was very angry. We talked about the time father and son had gone to Yellowstone and decided that No Entry signs were actually invitations to visit. Or the day Nils beat his father at chess but remained convinced his father had thrown the game. Nils's father kept asking me if I supported the war, and I kept telling him it didn't matter. He posed a different question: "After a man looks at these photographs, what, in his heart of hearts, do you want him to feel?" I said I wanted people to realize that these weren't just names and ranks of people who had died in a foreign place. I wanted people to feel the loss as one of our own. I wanted the dead to be remembered. Eventually, he gave me permission to photograph Nils's bedroom.

It happened again, three years later, in Canada. I was driving to visit a family when the father called to say he was with his ex-wife, and that I needed to speak to her. During our initial conversations, while I was in New York, he'd said that he hadn't yet spoken to his ex-wife about me, but that he would and there wouldn't be a problem. There was. When she got on the telephone, she was irritated. She told me no one had entered her son's room since he died. The door hadn't even been cracked, and there was no way a photographer was going in there if she couldn't bring herself to. I apologized as best I could but got her permission to call her back in twelve months.

On that same Canadian trip, I photographed Andrew Grenon's room in Windsor, Ontario, a frozen, windswept city across the river from Detroit. His father and mother had separated, and we'd arranged to meet together at his dad's place, where Andrew had lived before deploying to Afghanistan.

We all walked to Andrew's bedroom door, which his father opened. He motioned me in. I asked if he'd like to show me around, and he said he was fine where he was. He was unable to cross the threshold. Inside, it was as though Andrew had just left. Spare change lay on the floor by the bed, as though it had fallen out of his pocket as he put on a pair of jeans. Tossed over the end of the bed was a bathrobe. Andrew had showered, his dad told me, thrown on his army fatigues, and left for Afghanistan. That was the last time he saw him alive.

Most of the responses to the project were positive, and rarely did families give me a flat-out no. A handful of parents told me that it was not something they could do at the moment. They didn't give reasons, and I didn't ask. In 2010, Kathy Ryan, the director of photography of the *New York Times Magazine*, agreed to underwrite and publish a portion of the work, and I started introducing myself as Ashley Gilbertson from the *New York Times Magazine*. In some cases that changed the dynamic. On one occasion, I e-mailed a mother through Facebook, mentioning the *Times*. She wrote back forcefully, saying she hated the newspaper and its liberal editorial policies and had no interest in so much as a conversation.

I worked at various times with Austrian, Canadian, French, German, and Italian assistants to find families in their countries who would participate in this project. In Germany, we had had no success, and by the end of 2011 I'd given up. Fifty-three German soldiers had lost their lives in Afghanistan. Some of their families had made a pact to boycott the press. Moreover, the German military released little information about its causalities. But in January 2012, an old friend, Guido Mingels, who'd recently started work for the German newsweekly *Der Spiegel*, contacted me to say that a colleague had located a bedroom, and they planned a piece comparing the mourning process in Germany and the United States.

I flew to Stuttgart to meet Guido's colleague, Takis Würger, the reporter who had made contact with the family of Constantin Menz, a twenty-two-year-old soldier from the town of Backnang, just outside of Stuttgart. He had been shot by an Afghan soldier on Febuary 18, 2011.

Before meeting the family, Takis and I sat in a traditional German restaurant and talked into the night about the German military and the experience of its soldiers at home. Guido, Takis told me, had summed up the sentiment best: "In the United States, a dead soldier is a hero; in Germany, he's just a victim of war." German soldiers themselves were generally despised, Takis said. Germans, he explained, have a hard time differentiating between an Afghan deployment they generally oppose and the soldiers themselves. Their very presence reminds people of a time they'd rather forget.

Takis had embedded with soldiers in Afghanistan, and the stories he'd heard were astonishing. One soldier, home on leave in southern Germany, had gone to the train station, in uniform, to pick up his mother coming home from work. As he waited, a man disembarking from a train spat on him. Another soldier, a scout sniper, no less, told Takis he didn't dare wear his uniform in Berlin—it was simply too dangerous.

We visited Constantin Menz's family the following morning. His mother, Tanja, and father, Hans-Jürgen, greeted us warmly, and we discussed the project and learned about their son. Constantin had excelled at judo, a sport his younger sister, Janina, was still heavily involved in. He was in perfect shape and upon enlisting received a T1 on his physical, the highest grade possible, reserved for the best of the best. He could have done anything, and his mother thought he'd leave the army after a few weeks. But he fell in love with it and signed up for four years.

Tanja took us up to Constantin's room. She'd just returned his military effects to their place—a helmet and uniform, a pillow with medals pinned to it, and the folded German flag his family had been presented at the funeral. Tanja explained that a friend had come to stay, and she was worried the military items might make her feel uncomfortable as she slept in the dead child's room. The walls were plastered with Munch paintings, a map of Liberty City from the computer game Grand Theft Auto, and a poster for Him, the Finnish metal band. Tiny origami tanks gathered dust on the windowsill, gifts from Janina, his sister.

Janina, then seventeen, came home after she'd finished at school. She showed us a tattoo she'd gotten shortly after her brother died. It was a large orchid with her brother's nickname, Koni, under her heart. During summer break, Janina said, she worked as a lifeguard at the local pool. One day, someone approached her and asked who Koni was. "Just a friend," she'd said, too uncomfortable to explain that it was her brother because he had been a soldier, and he had died in Afghanistan.

When Constantin was killed, the town's mayor had trouble reaching out to the family. He didn't know what to say, Tanja told us. So she called him, and they arranged a meeting in the cemetery to discuss some type of memorial. Together, they looked at a small monument honoring "fallen heroes" of World War II. The word *hero* in Germany is poisoned by Nazism. "That won't do," Tanja told the mayor.

A second monument, to soldiers killed in World War I, was a large concrete marker with a cross in the middle. They agreed they would add Constantin Menz's name to that one.

"The flag in the U.S. is pride in country. It's comforting, something to fall back on. In Germany, we have nothing to fall back on," Takis said. "Half of our World Cup team refused to sing the national anthem."

• • •

Eighty-eight French troops died in Afghanistan before the last combat troops were withdrawn in November 2012. My French assistant, Julie Rasquin-Grucza, located the bedrooms of two whose parents had preserved them intact. Both families were immediately receptive to the project. Perhaps because of the "grand silence" surrounding their military—a virtual press blackout imposed by the army—the French seemed especially willing to talk to journalists.

Kevin Chassaing's mother, Marriette Guedon, heard just the basic premise of the proposal— that it's a memorial to the dead—before stopping Julie to ask, "What can I do for you?" Her son's room was as he had left it, she told Julie, and we could visit.

A month later, Julie and I were just outside of Bordeaux, on an old farm in a region known for its strawberries and tomatoes, sitting at a table with Marriette and her other son, Wilfred, drinking strong coffee and smoking. We were taken upstairs in the old farmhouse to Kevin's room. It was spacious and sparse—with the exception of his pocket knife collection, Kevin had little interest in material things, Marriette said. As a boy, he had a strong sense of moral justice and stood up for other kids being bullied at school.

A new, unworn white suit hung in his wardrobe. Kevin had planned on wearing it to his niece's baptism when he got home. His mother showed us his knives, neatly arranged above the fireplace. She recalled for us her final image of him. On Sunday, August 17, 2008, they were having a video chat on the computer, as they often did. Kevin was subdued in a way that was unlike him. "My baby, you don't smile for your Mama?" Marriette asked. He granted her wish and tried to explain away his dark mood: "I have to go out tomorrow," he said, "but it'll be okay."

The following day, Kevin's unit walked into a trap set by the Taliban thirty miles outside of Kabul. In what became known as the "Uzbin Valley ambush," nine French paratroopers were killed, another twenty-one wounded. At least one paratrooper was killed at close range with a knife, and some corpses were reportedly mutilated. Kevin was nineteen years old.

Several months later, Marriette was invited by the military to visit Forward Operating Base Tora, where her son had been stationed in Afghanistan. It's relatively common for European and Canadian families of the dead to be invited to the battlefield, though in the United States it's not an option. Families who have made the trip told me the journey helped them in their grief—it gave them a chance to connect to a part of their child's life that was otherwise closed to them. They ate what he ate, slept where he slept. They could see the landscape he patrolled, and where he played football with friends during downtime. They could also visit the stone memorials in the Afghan sand that their son's comrades had built.

Jean-Nicolas Panezyck was twenty-five when he died in Afghanistan alongside a comrade, a superior officer who was also shot dead trying to get him out of the line of fire after he'd been hit. His mother, Monique Panezyck, plans to make the trip when she's invited, after hearing from other mothers that there's a power in the place, that it had felt like their sons were somehow still there.

Julie and I spoke to Monique by Jean-Nicolas's grave in a cemetery surrounded by 1960s-era apartment complexes outside of Paris. Just beyond the buildings lay the glittering palaces of Versailles and the Longchamp Racecourse, but tourists never made it out here. It was about to rain, and we were the only ones in the graveyard. "If I die there," she said of the trip she planned to take, "at least I die on the same land as he did."

Monique raised Jean-Nicolas as a single mother, and he was her only child. When she met with us, she was out of hospital for the weekend. She was being treated for depression. "It's been six months," she told us, "but all I dream of is to follow him."

On weekdays, since her son was killed, she had been an inpatient at the hospital. She was being discharged every weekend to visit Jean-Nicolas's grave. Monique's apartment was only a few minutes' walk from the cemetery, and she liked being close to him.

In a recent phone call, Monique said therapy was helping her a lot, but when we'd sat together in her home, it wasn't helping in the slightest. Then, she would just sit in the therapist's chair and say, "Pourquoi? Pourquoi? Pourquoi?"—"Why? Why? Why?" Her words were labored; medications for depression slowed her speech. Between her words, I thought I recognized a silence and a stillness I had heard at only one other home, that of Jordan Haerter, in Sag Harbor, New York. Jordan was a Marine who had also grown up with his single working mother, and like Jean-Nicolas Panezyck he was an only child.

• • •

As of late 2013, eighty-one Italian servicemen have died in Iraq and Afghanistan. It proved easier to find preserved bedrooms in Italy than in other countries. Because of family custom and economic pressure, children live with their parents much longer in Italy. After contacting eleven families, my assistant, Alessandro Vecchi, had found four bedrooms belonging to fallen Italian soldiers.

Alessandro Pibiri—"Sandro" to his family—was twenty-four when he was killed by an improvised explosive device in southern Iraq in June 2006. He had volunteered to stay beyond his unit's allotted time to help with the transition to its successor in exchange for extra leave. Sandro planned to use his leave to go home to Sardinia, an Italian island in the Mediterranean known for its idyllic beaches, with a sheep population that outnumbers humans three to one.

My assistant and I visited Sandro's home in late August 2011. His room was perfectly preserved, down to the toy cars and cigarette lighters on his bookshelves. He'd lived with his parents, Marco and Luisella, in Selargius, a suburb of Sardinia's capital, Cagliari. On the island, where they call the Italian mainland the "Continent," residents were guarded toward outsiders. It was a testament to my assistant's gentle approach that we'd been invited to meet the parents and discuss the project with them.

Sandro's parents listened carefully as we sat at the kitchen table and explained the project. After about an hour they started telling us about their son. He was very close to his parents, sharing everything about his life, down to intimate details like his concern about a girlfriend's late cycle. He drove his car slower than any other teenager in the area, Marco said, because he was always hanging out the window greeting people.

At one point, Sandro's mother stood and gathered photo albums from a closet in his bedroom. She put them on the table and showed us baby photos of her son, snapshots of him growing up, Sandro and his father at the beach, family dinners. In the pictures, he grew older quickly. He developed into a teenager, went to high school, posing for the camera with a big boisterous smile among groups of friends. All of a sudden, he was a young man. He stood proudly in front of a new car. Soon after came pictures of Sandro at the airport, dressed in fatigues.

The family was seeing him off to Afghanistan. Luisella told us that she'd managed to remain strong during the sendoff, though Marco had started crying. Sandro pulled his mother aside and whispered that he'd never seen his father cry before.

Marco, who'd been quiet until then, was overcome by emotion. He threw a pencil and eraser he'd been toying with onto the tabletop; they came to a stop by a book of sudoku puzzles. "It was the last time I saw him," he said, his voice breaking.

Luisella was still looking at the pictures in the album. "I'm stuck at that point, right there," she said, looking at the photos of them at the airport. "I'm waiting for him to come home."

The rest of the pages in the album were blank.

I have seen photographs and videos like those in homes around the world. Generally, mothers and fathers dote on their sons at the airport, hugging them when they're supposed to be standing next to them for photos. The young men seldom look comfortable. Their youthful awkwardness usually gets the better of their newfound military poise, and they try to comfort their parents, a hand on a back, a look to the side, not really knowing what to say.

Zachary Clouser's mother, Deb, had showed me a video a relative made of her at the airport. She hugs her son tightly, and he hugs her back affectionately. Zach was a comic, sometimes mischievous, and in the video he rolls his eyes and grins. They break their embrace. As he prepares to leave, his mother hugs him again. This time he hugs her back, not kidding around. They part, and this time Debra is crying.

I don't remember the precise moment or place I first saw scenes like that play out in person. I do, however, vividly recall being at an airport somewhere in the United States after photographing a bedroom. It was your standard departure hall: high ceilings, banks of screens listing ETAs and ETDs, neutral-colored walls, glass. People rushing in every direction, a shoe-shine station, fast-food counters, gate changes and last calls announced over the public address system.

Amidst it all, I saw a family. They were making those pictures together, a uniformed son surrounded. The mother was crying, and every time the parents tried to leave, she'd run back and hug him again. He was going to war, I didn't need to ask to know that. As I watched, the airport's noise and movement felt suspended. I thought that moment would be a great photo essay, saying goodbye. But then I thought of the families for whom it would be the last goodbye. I sat down and wept.

Luisella put the albums of her son Sandro on a bench behind her, and we were invited to visit his room. I began working on the photograph, while my assistant continued conversation with the family at the table.

Another Italian family, the parents of Luigi Pascazio, had lost their son in Afghanistan. A few days earlier, his father, a police officer, had expressed his grief this way: "Parents who have a criminal child are luckier. They can at least visit him in prison. I will never see Luigi again."

In Sardinia, after Sandro finished middle school, he had earned a diploma as a window fitter. He couldn't find work in the depressed economy, though, so joined the army instead. Requests for bids still sometimes come in the mail, and occasionally, his mother said, the phone rings with a builder looking to hire him.

"No," she tells them. "It's too late."

• • •

I wish the book could end here, that we could look at the forty bedrooms knowing combat had long since ended, imagine the lives of those who lived there, mourn their loss, and say, That's done. It was tragic but it's finished—U.S. and coalition troops are out of Iraq and Afghanistan. But for some who served there, the wars will never end.

The bedrooms here belonged, with one exception, to men and women killed in theater. By early 2013 the United States had lost well over 6,000 service members during twelve years in Iraq and Afghanistan. But each year, the nation loses more veterans to suicide: 6,600, by Department of Veteran Affairs estimates—an average of eighteen veterans every day. It's a harrowing fact, but what's more harrowing is that many of those deaths are preventable.

In 2007, on a freezing day in May, I attended a Memorial Day ceremony in Minnesota. A World War II veteran stood in front of the small crowd at a cemetery in Virginia, Minnesota, and talked about Iraq and Afghanistan. He asked the crowd not to forget those who won't be coming home, before breaking down and crying at the lectern. He started speaking of friends who had died more than half a century before, about how he might have done things differently. Then he stopped, unable to continue, and left the podium. Back then they called it shell shock.

Post-traumatic stress disorder, as it is now officially diagnosed, is not an obvious physical wound. The pain of PTSD doesn't lessen over time. Only with proper therapy can those afflicted by it learn to carry on. Unit commanders are responsible for looking after troops in war, and the Department of Veteran Affairs is responsible for taking care of them when they come home. Yet the VA is underfunded, understaffed, and short on expertise about PTSD treatment. As it stands, those desperately needing help are sometimes turned away.

Ryan Yurchison was one of those people. He'd served a tour in Iraq and was wrestling with his trauma when he died of an overdose on May 22, 2010, in Youngstown, Ohio. His family and friends are certain it was suicide.

Ryan was twenty-four years old when he was stationed at a base in southwest Baghdad. On September 14, 2006, he was assigned to search dump trucks at the base's gate. He was not provided with tools to search the mountains of dirt they carried, and just after midday he allowed another truck onto the base. Thirty seconds later, the truck exploded, killing three soldiers and wounding thirty more, Ryan himself included.

As part of the treatment for his physical pain, Ryan was put on a course of Vicodin and Percocet. Those drugs did nothing, though, to lessen the guilt he felt for the deaths of the three soldiers, and Ryan suffered alone, unable to confide in comrades, friends, or family.

In Germany, and later in Ohio, he appeared fine to those around him, but to VA doctors he complained of nightmares and being unable to sleep for days on end. He was formally diagnosed with PTSD and prescribed more painkillers and additional medications for anxiety and depression.

Living once again in his childhood home, in New Middletown, Ohio, he had his prescriptions replenished by mail. The care he needed—consistent therapy provided by a qualified professional—wasn't available to him. After two years, the VA noticed Ryan was requesting refills before his prescriptions were supposed to run out, and they cut him off from the most potent drugs.

Addicted now, he turned to buying pills on the street.

Ryan was an amateur filmmaker, and around this time he made a short depicting himself in bed, tossing and turning, unable to sleep. In the film, he gets up, drinks a beer, and sits watching a television screen filled only with static. Then he puts a noose around his neck and simulates hanging himself. Ryan uploaded the video to YouTube, where his mother, Cherry, saw it. She called the VA, desperate, and begged for help.

An appointment was made with a physician, who advised Ryan to take his prescribed medications and to read an "anxiety and phobia workbook."

By February 2010, Ryan's symptoms had worsened. He was heavily self-medicating, barely sleeping, and having nightmares when he did. He became aggressive. Cherry persuaded him to return to the VA, this time to seek in-patient treatment for addiction and post-traumatic stress. Ryan was told they would be unable to place him for another four to six months.

In the weeks that followed, Ryan's childhood friend and battle buddy in Iraq, Steve, attempted suicide. While Steve was in the hospital, Ryan's drug use accelerated. On May 21, 2010, a Friday, Ryan drove half an hour to the Royal Oaks, a local bar where he was a regular. He knocked back Xanibombs—Jägermeister with crushed Xanax mixed into it—chased down with Pabst Blue Ribbons and handfuls of benzos. Between midnight and 2:00 a.m., Ryan called dozens of friends. No one picked up. The behavior was unlike him. The calls might have been a plea for help, though his friend Steve is certain Ryan was calling to say goodbye.

At 2:30 a.m., Ryan went to his dealer's house, five minutes from the bar. "He was staggering, just totally messed up," the dealer recalled. "I ain't never seen him like that. Never." Ryan said he was upset and wanted to kill himself. The dealer had heard this before and persuaded Ryan to stay and sleep it off.

The following morning, the dealer's girlfriend found Ryan face down on a pile of cushions. He was dead.

The police reported the death as an accidental overdose. His friends and family believe Ryan killed himself.

His mother, Cherry, blames the VA's unresponsiveness for her son's death. "The military takes these guys, uses them, and then sends them home as damaged goods without doing enough, if anything, to help them. Ryan's death was preventable and treatments exist, but veterans aren't getting the help they deserve."

We were sitting on her front porch. To our right was Ryan's darkened bedroom. We'd just come from there. When we'd entered, Cherry had walked straight to a space by the foot of her son's bed and picked up a crumpled T-shirt. Ryan had used it to wipe away tears on the night he died, she said. She put the shirt to her nose and inhaled her son's scent.

ACKNOWLEDGMENTS

To all of the families who embraced me with warmth and trust, thank you for making one of the most difficult projects I've ever worked on inspiring and moving.

Thank you to my family, my wife, Joanna, and my son, Hugo; to my parents, Wendy and Peter Gilbertson; to my aunt and uncle, Fiona and Peter Barber; to the parents of LCPL William Miller, Susie and Lewis Miller; to my editor at the *New York Times Magazine*, Kathy Ryan; to my editor at the University of Chicago Press, Alan Thomas; to the designer of this book, Matt Avery, and its manuscript editor, Joel Score; to my web designer and assistant, Martin Fuchs; to the Aaron Siskind Foundation for its 2010 grant; to David Hazan and the staff of Print Space NYC for brilliant post-production; to my agent and his assistant, Michael Carlisle and Lauren Smythe at Inkwell Management; to Philip Gourevich for his powerful introduction; to the staff and photographers of VII Photo; to Guido Mingels and Takis Wuerger; and to my translators, producers, and assistants, Julie Rasquin Grucza, Camiel Bulder, Marla Ulrich, Alessandro Vecchi, Riley Sparks, Adam McCauley, and Haley Hamblin.

And thank you to all of the backers who contributed to this project on Kickstarter: Melissa Allan, Jason Andrew and Julie Hau, Auria European Chamber Orchestra, Elizabeth Bagot and Arthur Huh, Marla H. Bane and Michael L. Benson, Fiona Barber, Richard Beaven, Chynita Belcher, Mike Berube, Travis Betz, Cathy Brinkorth, Michael Christopher Brown, Camiel Bulder, Peter Carey and Frances Coady, Michelle Rabinowitz Carney, David Chen, Meagan Cignoli, Philip Colicchio, Jennine Collier, Jessica Coville, Andrew Curtis, Benny Czap, Jim Daniels, Annie Dorsen, Lucy Dowling, Carolyn Drake, Phil Dudouit, Carl Dziunka, Rob Edwards, Chris and Meagan Eller, L. J. and Ginger Emerson, Charlie and Karen Fredrickson, Martin Fuchs, Alice Gabriner, Claudia Ganz, Marcela Gaviria, the Gianforte family, Peter Gilbertson, Matthew Goddard-Jones, Michael Goldfarb, Ben Greenland, Julie and Tim Grucza, Carol Gunby, Brett Gundlock, David Guttenfelder, Matt, Anita, and Lucia Hall, Claire Halliday, Cara Hammer, David Koji Kariyado Hansen, David Alan Harvey, Christine Hauser and Warzer Jaff, Ron Haviv, Steven L. Hawkins, Katja Heinemann, Shannon Hourigan, Anthony Howells, Paul Jeffers, Krisanne Johnson, C. J. Johnson, Whitney C. Johnson, Ed Kashi, Jessica Kaye, Katie Khouri, Garrett Kiely, Pete Knicke, Steven Koves, Stella Kramer, Colleen Krenzer, Rose Krueger, Lowy Lacar, Samyukta Lakshmi, Rick Langenbrunner, Boots Levinson, Lance Cory Lobo, Amanda Lucier, Melissa Lyttle, Peter Maass, Judith Marinoff, Gina Martin, Ssgt. and Mrs. Kyle Mastropasqua, Mary Beth Meehan, Nancy Meis, Susan Meiselas, Nalis Merelli, Alexander Millet,

Kyle Mohen, Shannon Morris, Meredith G. Morton, Naomi Mullumby, Jehad Nga, Landon Nordeman, Lu Olkowski, Ron Osgood, David Dare Parker, Sheri Pasquarella, Joseph Pearson, Sam Phelps, Jon Plasse, Nick Poggioli, Katell Pommereul, Leslie Powell, Jamie Powell, Bill Putnam, Espen Rasmussen, Rob Ray, Samantha Reinders, Melissa Riggs, Alan Rowlette, S. J. Rozan, J. D. Ryan, Rolando Sanchez, Suzanne Santos, Sarah Schuster and Kalin Rachev, Naomi Schegloff, Anthony Schroeder, Jeff Sheinkopf, Joao Silva, Stephanie Sinclair, Jared Soares, Lesley Sparks, Brodie Standen, John Stanmeyer, Art Stevens, Still Waters in a Storm, Andrea Taverna, Alan Thomas, Hannah Tometzki, Kris Torgeson, Erin Trieb, Jeffrey Trunell, James Turnbull, Matt Tyrnauer, Peter van Agtmael, Tomas van Houtryve, Stephen Voss, Julian Wainwright, Gloria Ware, Liz Warren, Dennis Weaver, Nathan Webster, Rick Winfield, and Ken Wohlrob.

In addition to the people listed above, there are many others who have helped me in the seven years I've been working on *Bedrooms of The Fallen*. You know who you are. I thank you all.